THE LEARNING POWER OF LISTENING

A Practical Guide for Using SenseMaker

Authors:
Irene Guijt, Oxfam Great Britain (Head of Evidence and Strategic Learning)
www.oxfam.org.uk
Maria Veronica Gottret, Catholic Relief Service (Senior Technical Advisor for Agriculture and Livelihoods Research) www.crs.org
Anna Hanchar, The Data Atelier
www.thedataatelier.com
Steff Deprez, Voices that Count
www.voicesthatcount.net
Rita Muckenhirn, Systways
www.systways.com

Editors:
Solveig Bang, Cecilia Sorra

© 2022 Catholic Relief Services and Oxfam

Practical Action Publishing Ltd
25 Albert Street, Rugby, CV21 2SD,
Warwickshire, UK
www.practicalactionpublishing.org

9781788531993 Hardback
9781788531986 Paperback
9781788532006 PDF

Guijt, I., Gottret, MA., Hanchar, A., Deprez, S., Muckenhirn, R., (2022) *The Learning Power of Listening*, Rugby, UK: Practical Action Publishing <http://dx.doi.org/10.3362/9781788532006>.

Although the authors and publishers have made every effort to ensure that the information in this guidance was correct at press time, the authors and publishers make no warranties of any kind and do not assume and hereby disclaim any liability to any party for any loss, damage, or disruption caused by errors or omissions, whether such errors or omissions result from negligence, accident, or any other cause.

The intention of this guide is to share good practice and guidance on an approach to inquiry as it is used in development practice. The authors alone are responsible for the views expressed in this guide which do not necessarily represent the views, decisions or policies of the institutions with which they are affiliated, nor those of The Cynefin Company.

This publication is copyrighted but may be reproduced for personal use for the purposes of education and research, but only if the source is acknowledged in full. For reproduction in any other circumstances, or for reuse in other publications, or for distribution, public display, translation, modification or adaptation, permission must be secured and a fee may be charged. Email pqpublications@crs.org and policyandpractice@oxfam.org.uk.

Photos:
Rita Muckenhirn & Catholic Relief Services
Design:
RCO Design

Catholic Relief Services is the official international humanitarian agency of the United States Catholic community. CRS' relief and development work is accomplished through programs of emergency response, HIV, health, agriculture, education, microfinance, and peacebuilding. CRS eases suffering and provides assistance to people in need in more than a hundred countries, without regard to race, religion, or nationality.

Catholic Relief Services
228 West Lexington Street
Baltimore, MD 21201-3443 USA
1.888.277.7575 | www.crs.org

Oxfam works with partner organizations and alongside vulnerable women and men to end the injustices that cause poverty.
Oxfam's work saves lives and helps rebuild livelihoods when crisis strikes. It campaigns so that the voices of people living in poverty influence the local and global decisions that affect them.

Oxfam Great Britain
John Smith Drive
Oxford OX4 2JY United Kingdom
+44 (0) 1865 472602
www.oxfam.org.uk

Reviewers

CRS Reviewers
Clara Hagens, John Hembling, Marianna Hensley, Amy Hilleboe, Mohit Holmesheoran, Dennis Latimer, Juan Alberto Molina, Andrés Montenegro, Peter Mureithi, Jean Nyemba, Matthew Peckarsky, Guy Sharrock, Matthew Will, Maria Josephine Wijiastuti

Oxfam Great Britain reviewers
Sabita Banerji, Simone Lombardini, Franziska Mager, Alexia Petria, Rebecca Smith

Introducing SenseMaker

- 13 Complexity and a Changing Landscape
- 16 What Sensemaker is and How it Works
- 17 Key Features of Sensemaker
- 25 The Sensemaker Process
- 25 Deciding to Use SenseMaker
- 26 Phase 1: Preparation for the SenseMaker process
- 26 Phase 2: Design of the Signification Framework
- 27 Phase 3: Collection of Narratives and Facilitation of their Self-Signification
- 28 Phase 4: Sensemaking with Stakeholders
- 29 The Software

Suitability Assessment

- 31 Comparing Sensemaker to Common Methods of Inquiry
- 34 Becoming Acquainted with the Sensemaker Method
- 37 Criteria to Assess the Suitability of Sensemaker

More

- 6 Acronyms and Abbreviations
- 7 Boxes and Figures
- 8 Tables
- 9 About This Guide
- 10 Glossary
- 182 Epilogue: Why We Wrote This Guide
- 190 References & Further Reading

Phase 1: Preparation

- 41 Core Decisions about the SenseMaker Process
- 43 Main Considerations
- 49 Ethical Considerations
- 51 Developing the Sensemaker Process Plan

Phase 2: Design

- 55 Signification Framework Design Principles
- 57 The Analytical Framing of the Sensemaker Process
- 61 Designing the Sampling Strategy
- 64 Design and Structure of the Signification Framework
- 66 Drafting the Signification Framework
- 86 Testing and Critically Reviewing the Signification Framework
- 90 Creating and Testing the Digital Version of the Signification Framework
- 91 Translating the Signification Framework

Phase 3: Collection

- 93 Collection Scenarios
- 94 Collection Principles
- 96 Ethics During the Collection Process
- 97 How to Collect Data Step-by-Step
- 97 Step 1: Preparing for Collection
- 104 Step 2: Training Facilitators and Conducting Final User Testing
- 107 Step 3: Facilitating the Collection Process
- 118 Step 4: Monitoring Collection and Ensuring Data Quality

Phase 4: Sensemaking

- 124 Sensemaking Principles
- 125 Deciding on the Sensemaking Strategy
- 129 Preparing for Sensemaking
- 131 Building Block 1: Primary Analysis
- 158 Building Block 2: Collective Interpretation
- 168 Building Block 3: Comprehensive Analysis
- 178 Building Block 4: Communication and Use

Acronyms and Abbreviations

A3B	Applying the 3Bs (binding, bonding, bridging)
CAR	Central African Republic
CRS	Catholic Relief Services
CSV	comma separated value (.csv file format)
DFID	Department for International Development
ETI	Ethical Trading Initiative
ID	identification
IFAD	International Fund for Agricultural Development
IHD	Integral Human Development
IT	information technology
KDE	kernel density estimation
MCQ	multiple-choice question
M&E	monitoring and evaluation
MEAL	monitoring, evaluation, accountability, and learning
N/A	not applicable
NGO	nongovernmental organization
OVC	orphans and vulnerable children
SILC	Savings and Internal Lending Communities
SMART	specific, measurable, attainable, relevant, and time-bound indicators
TOR	terms of reference
UK	United Kingdom
UNDP	United Nations Development Programme
US	United States
USAID	United States Agency for International Development

Boxes

14 **Box 1.** Using SenseMaker to understand the causes of impact trends
15 **Box 2.** Using SenseMaker to understand underlying structures and mental models
16 **Box 3.** Identifying unknown unknowns with SenseMaker
17 **Box 4.** Example of a SenseMaker narrative
39 **Box 5.** Questions to ask before deciding to use SenseMaker
50 **Box 6.** Example of ethical principles for research
68 **Box 7.** Examples from practice to frame the design
88 **Box 8.** Checklist of questions for testing a draft signification framework
102 **Box 9.** Tasks to prepare devices for collection
108 **Box 10.** Explaining a triad question in online collection
154 **Box 11.** Difficult life conditions – a narrative from a female agricultural worker in northern Africa
170 **Box 12.** Different ways of using narratives in comprehensive analysis
175 **Box 13.** Using visualizations to explore relationships between two variables
181 **Box 14.** Channels to communicate SenseMaker findings

Figures

18 **Figure 1.** Self-signification process using the body, pen and paper, or a tablet
20 **Figure 2.** Slider signifier question enabling nuanced answer between two extremes
21 **Figure 3.** Signifier question comparing several people's perspectives
22 **Figure 4.** Signifier question (triad) giving wider relevance of a single story
23 **Figure 5.** Signifier question (triad) highlighting a minor story cluster
24 **Figure 6.** Signifier question (triad) indicating the desired pattern during the program's lifespan
25 **Figure 7.** Phases of a SenseMaker process
58 **Figure 8.** CRS analytical framework developed to assess 'pathways to prosperity' and resilience capabilities
64 **Figure 9.** Process of designing the signification framework (new or adapting an existing one)
87 **Figure 10.** Changing the review focus at different stages of the signification framework design
96 **Figure 11.** When to consider ethics
114 **Figure 12.** Screenshot of a canvas with stones
120 **Figure 13.** Concentrated and spread response patterns
123 **Figure 14.** Components of the sensemaking phase
156 **Figure 15.** Visualizing the most frequently used words
168 **Figure 16.** Responses to migration as a coping mechanism when faced with a shock or stressor (Gottret 2017)
169 **Figure 17.** The analysis pathway: role of migration
171 **Figure 18.** Qualitative analysis of narratives: word tree. (CRS, Nicaragua)
172 **Figure 19.** Respondents' progression along a 'pathway to prosperity'
173 **Figure 20.** Post-categorization of trajectories along a 'pathway to prosperity' (CRS, Nicaragua)
174 **Figure 21.** Exploring the relationship between two variables
175 **Figure 22.** Examples of density plots: contour and heat maps
176 **Figure 23.** Exploring the relationship between two variables: XY plot
176 **Figure 24.** Exploring the relationship between two variables: contour plot
176 **Figure 25.** Filtering a slider question by the pathway followed

Tables

- 32 **Table 1.** Comparing SenseMaker with other methods of inquiry
- 34 **Table 2.** Examples of SenseMaker studies
- 42 **Table 3.** Examples of core team decision domains and responsibilities
- 46 **Table 4.** Example of main budget items by phase and activity
- 52 **Table 5.** Checklist for developing a timeline for the SenseMaker process
- 62 **Table 6.** Sampling strategies and their implications for sensemaking
- 65 **Table 7.** Overview of question types for signification frameworks
- 70 **Table 8.** Examples and purposes of prompters.
- 71 **Table 9.** Examples of title questions
- 72 **Table 10.** Variations, design recommendations, and data format generated for slider questions
- 72 **Table 11.** Examples of slider signifier questions
- 74 **Table 12.** Variations, design recommendations, and data format generated for slider-with-stones questions
- 76 **Table 13.** Examples of slider-with-stones signifier questions
- 78 **Table 14.** Variations, design recommendations and data format generated for canvas-with-stones questions
- 79 **Table 15.** Examples of canvas-with-stones signifier questions
- 80 **Table 16.** Variations, design recommendations, and data format generated for triad questions
- 82 **Table 17.** Examples of triad signifier questions by purpose
- 82 **Table 18.** Examples of context-specific versus generic triad signifier questions
- 84 **Table 19.** Design recommendations and data format generated for multiple-choice questions
- 85 **Table 20.** Examples of signifier MCQs
- 102 **Table 21.** Checklist to prepare for collection
- 105 **Table 22.** Facilitator competencies for collecting narratives and self-signification
- 106 **Table 23.** Training content for the four competencies
- 111 **Table 24.** Encouraging respondents to share a narrative
- 113 **Table 25.** Facilitating a slider signifier question
- 115 **Table 26.** Facilitating a canvas-with-stones signifier question
- 117 **Table 27.** Facilitating a triad signifier question
- 127 **Table 28.** Software options for visualization and analysis
- 138 **Table 29.** Tips and recommendations for analyzing slider questions using The Cynefin Company's proprietary software
- 140 **Table 30.** Examples of types of slider signifier questions
- 141 **Table 31.** Tips and recommendations for analyzing slider-with-stones questions using The Cynefin Company's proprietary software
- 142 **Table 32.** Examples of types of slider-with-stones signifier questions
- 145 **Table 33.** Tips and recommendations for analyzing canvas-with-stones signifier questions using The Cynefin Company's proprietary software
- 146 **Table 34.** Examples of types of canvas-with-stones signifier questions
- 148 **Table 35.** Tips and recommendations for analyzing triad questions using The Cynefin Company's proprietary software
- 150 **Table 36.** Examples of analyzing different triad signifier questions
- 153 **Table 37.** Examples of context-specific and generic triad signifier questions
- 160 **Table 38.** Examples of different ways to structure collective interpretation
- 164 **Table 39.** Template for planning the content of collective interpretation events
- 174 **Table 40.** Signification framework questions to explore link between effects of loans and savings and levels of self-sufficiency

About this guide

The Learning Power of Listening guide is intended for those who wish to coordinate, participate in, or support the use of SenseMaker—a complexity-aware, narrative-based method—in conducting assessments, monitoring progress, and carrying out evaluations or research. The guide can be used for personal reference or for training others involved in a SenseMaker process.

The experiences on which the guide is based, as well as the examples used, focus mainly on development programs, and particularly on efforts that focus on poverty reduction, social justice, peacebuilding, resilience, behavioral change, and restoring and protecting natural resources. They come from organizations and programs that have used SenseMaker over the last decade.

The guide starts with considerations for judging the suitability of the method, followed by descriptions of the four phases of any SenseMaker process. Besides detailed guidance on preparing for and implementing a SenseMaker process, examples, and advice are offered for each phase. Despite its practical focus, this is not a do-it-yourself guide: there is no shortcut to learning SenseMaker. Mastering its practice requires deep, hands-on involvement in at least one to two processes from start to finish. Guidance from an experienced SenseMaker practitioner is also recommended.

The guide summarizes practices that have evolved in international development, providing practical tips and examples of context-specific adaptations. However, as with any method, SenseMaker needs to be adapted to each application and context, and each process will be different. The purpose, topic of interest, learning questions, competencies of the core team and facilitators, financial resources, and time frame will all influence the decisions and approaches taken.

The Introducing SenseMaker chapter outlines the growing awareness of complexity in international development, providing fertile ground for the emergence of greater interest in the method. The main features of SenseMaker are discussed, followed by a summary of the phases and main steps of a SenseMaker process. The introductory chapter also includes a section on Suitability Assessment, which discusses what to consider when deciding whether to use SenseMaker.

The details of each phase of a SenseMaker process are then discussed in the four subsequent chapters:

- Phase 1: Preparation
- Phase 2: Design
- Phase 3: Collection
- Phase 4: Sensemaking

Glossary

SenseMaker uses novel terminology to describe its unique process and question types. Such terms can help newcomers to the method let go of their existing thinking about and practices for conducting evaluations, research, and analysis. All the terms listed here are discussed in more detail in the guide.

Analytical framing The set of concepts, theory of change, or analytical framework used to design the signification framework and guide the sensemaking process.

Canvas with stones One type of SenseMaker core follow-up question or signifier, where respondents place different options, called 'stones', on a two-by-two matrix of continuums that represent related but distinct elements of a concept.

Collector The Cynefin Company's proprietary software for browser-based (online) or app-based (online and offline) data entry.

Core SenseMaker questions Questions specific to the SenseMaker method.

Dashboard A tool on the SenseMaker platform that gives an aggregate view of the signification data and simple patterns.

Data Exporter SenseMaker Suite functionality for accessing and downloading datasets.

Dataset An organized collection of narratives and self-signification data.

Designer A SenseMaker Suite functionality for digital configuration of signification frameworks.

Facilitators Team of contractors or volunteers who facilitate the collection process and conduct the interviews.

Filter A function of responses to multiple-choice questions (MCQs) that allows disaggregation of the data for analysis and comparison between subsets of respondents.

Gaming In surveys, 'gaming' refers to respondents selecting a response that does not accurately reflect the situation, in order to obtain a benefit from the program (e.g. to be selected as a project participant or to receive services from a project), or to please the facilitator or organization conducting the study.

Heat map A representation of data in the form of a plot, in which data are presented in a system of color-coding to visualize the concentration of responses.

Local dataset Dataset downloaded via Data Exporter functionality of the SenseMaker Suite.

Master dataset The original dataset stored online. Accessible via Data Exporter functionality of the SenseMaker Suite.

Narrative Prompted by an open-ended question, a 'narrative' is a respondent's spoken or written account of connected events about a real-life experience.

Outlier Refers to a response that is outside a dominant pattern or large cluster of responses. Outliers in SenseMaker may be weak signals of a practice or situation that a program may wish to stimulate, or a threat or undesirable effect that the program may wish to reduce.

Prompter An open-ended question used to generate or trigger the sharing of a narrative that includes an account of connected events about a real-life experience.

Scatter plot Refers to two types of plots: a) plots displaying responses to core SenseMaker signifier questions, and b) plots displaying two variables across two axes showing association between them.

Self-signification The process by which respondents answer predefined follow-up questions about a real-life experience they shared in the narrative, allowing additional layers of information to be collected.

SenseMaker core team The team responsible for the design and implementation of the SenseMaker process from start to finish.

SenseMaker lead The person overseeing the whole SenseMaker process.

SenseMaker Suite A secure Cynefin Company portal that allows personalized access to a range of functionalities allowing the digital configuration of signification frameworks, modifying and downloading datasets, visualizing and summarizing the data.

SenseMaker process The process of implementing a SenseMaker-based assessment, monitoring, evaluation (baseline, midterm, or final), or research study from start to finish.

SenseMaker process plan A document designed to guide the SenseMaker process from start to finish, which includes the purpose, learning or research questions, implementation plan, roles and responsibilities, budget, and a communication plan.

SenseMaker trainer and facilitator A person qualified to train and facilitate the design, collection, and sensemaking phases of a SenseMaker process. This should be a skilled SenseMaker practitioner with good facilitation skills.

Sensemaking The process of describing, summarizing, analyzing, making sense of, and communicating data and emerging knowledge to make decisions and act on the findings. It has four components: (1) primary analysis, (2) collective interpretation, (3) comprehensive analysis, and (4) communication and use.

Signification framework The core SenseMaker collection tool, equivalent to a survey instrument. Includes a prompter, a story title question, a set of core SenseMaker follow-up questions or signifiers, and a set of questions on sociodemographics and collection protocol.

Signifier question Core SenseMaker questions used to capture additional layers of information about the narrative shared by the respondent. The types of signifier questions are multiple-choice questions (MCQ), triads, sliders, sliders with stones, and canvas with stones.

Slider One type of SenseMaker core follow-up question or signifier, where respondents place their response on a line between two extremes.

Slider with stones One type of SenseMaker core follow-up question or signifier, where respondents place different options, called 'stones', on a line between two extremes.

Title question An open-ended question that elicits a few key words that describe the respondent's experience of personal significance shared in the narrative.

Triad One type of SenseMaker core follow-up question or signifier, where respondents reflect on the relative importance of three different elements related to a single concept in their narrative.

Workbench Workbench is a tool on the SenseMaker platform that allows in-depth exploration of patterns through statistical analysis.

Introducing SenseMaker

- 13 Complexity and a Changing Landscape
- 16 What SenseMaker is and How it Works
- 17 Key Features of SenseMaker
- 25 The SenseMaker Process
- 25 Deciding to Use SenseMaker
- 26 Phase 1: Preparation for the SenseMaker process
- 26 Phase 2: Design of the Signification Framework
- 27 Phase 3: Collection of Narratives and Facilitation of their Self-Signification
- 28 Phase 4: Sensemaking with Stakeholders
- 29 The Software

Working with complex change processes requires an adaptive approach to change, with continual probing, making sense of evolving situations, adjusting actions, and learning.

Introducing SenseMaker

Complexity and a Changing Landscape

Every year, those involved in working to reduce poverty and inequality try to plan more effectively, use lessons they have learned, consult more, and explain transformational processes more clearly. Yet at the end of each year, reports detail unplanned activities and justifications of why planned activities did not turn out as expected — or were not implemented at all. Practitioners wrestle with the constant contradiction between implementing feasible solutions, meeting contractually binding work plans with predefined indicators and targets, and adjusting strategies and actions in response to evolving needs and changing contexts. They must deal with the inevitability of complexity.

Complexity is present in many ways. The uncertainty caused by the continually evolving needs and interests of stakeholders collides with the unpredictable effect of changes in local and national leadership and their implications for public investment priorities, practices, and policies. In many contexts, security risks present additional operational risks and unknowns, while the insidious effects of long-term environmental stresses are being felt in ever more livelihoods. Complexity is present even in seemingly simple scenarios, such as those that seek to introduce a technology known to work elsewhere, such as malaria nets, or to provide a well-established service, such as primary school education. How change happens is influenced by many factors, including social and personal norms, historical precedence, private sector practices, public policies, and existing capabilities. This inevitably makes even so-called 'simple changes' and known solutions complex. Complex processes hinge on changes that are unpredictable and on cause–effect relationships that are not straightforward, and where progress is determined by ongoing and emerging efforts. Truly understanding such processes of change is often only possible in retrospect; outcomes cannot be predicted accurately or confidently.

Working with complex change processes requires an adaptive approach to change, with continual probing, making sense of evolving situations, adjusting actions, and learning. Accountability is not only about outcomes, which cannot be predicted or guaranteed: it is also about demonstrating how collaboration, learning, and adaptation have led to ever better practices and have contributed to impact. Adaptive responses require the ability to generate insights in real time about emerging conditions and about what works and what does not. Insights from the people whose lives are the focus of change efforts are essential for effective adaptation and improvement. People need to probe promising practices or respond to new options—and then observe, look for patterns, interpret, understand, and value the response to the actions that have been taken (Snowden and Boone 2007).

However, most monitoring, evaluation, accountability, and learning (MEAL) methods to date are not adept at producing insights when operating in complex situations or on complex change processes. Complexity-aware planning methods, such as SenseMaker, explicitly explore and analyze data patterns by involving many stakeholders in the interpretation process. Involving more people can lead to better insights for continual strategic reflection, learning, adaptation, and accountability. This will enable development organizations to move from conventional methods to a process that fosters collaborative learning and adaptive management.

Being able to deal with the complexity of context and of change processes requires observations to be understood better and more deeply. Probing into patterns and trends provides important nuances, lifting the lid on factors behind puzzling results (see Box 1). These patterns can also help shed light on the structures and mental models that explain the reasons for observed events and phenomena (see Box 2). Such depth can improve the likelihood of identifying appropriate solutions, leading to more innovation in practice.

Box 1 describes an application in 2015 based on a scenario that is common in many organizations. It reflects deeply rooted and widespread disconnects between how

Box 1.

Using SenseMaker to understand the causes of impact trends

After an external midterm evaluation, Catholic Relief Services (CRS) in Nicaragua reflected on the results with the project team. Analysis of the MEAL data had shown that only vegetable producers located on better-endowed lands, and who possessed more resources, could increase productivity and were on track to reach the targets. Livestock and bean producers, on the other hand, showed stagnant or reduced productivity levels, respectively. The data collected using conventional MEAL did not show which factors led to these results, or whether and how the project had contributed to these outcomes. CRS staff and partners found it difficult to understand why productivity had increased or decreased.

The SenseMaker process made it possible for staff to look into underlying causes, by listening to multiple voices and perspectives. Farmers who had shared experiences that they felt should be avoided in future mentioned both credit and climate risks (drought or unpredictable rainfall during the cropping season) as key factors. In addition to losing their crops, farmers were left paying off debts. They were forced to sell assets, severely affecting their livelihoods and leaving them prey to a vicious cycle of debt.

Climate risks and the limited resilience of smallholders needed further inquiry and action. The study showed that agricultural intensification was a risky strategy, with some positive results but also negative outcomes. These findings led the program team to design new projects that focused on soil and water restoration and protection, to help farmers adapt to increasingly serious climate risks. The new design also included financial education and promotion of savings, rather than solely focusing on access to credit (Gottret et al. 2017).

change happens, how implementing organizations support change processes, how these processes are assessed, and how this supports learning. The example shows how SenseMaker helped step beyond the limitations of common practice.

To be effective, programs need to be designed and implemented based on in-depth local assessments of complex operating environments. These assessments need to take account of the underlying structures and mental models that cause the symptoms. SenseMaker offers an effective approach (see Box 2), which is a challenge using conventional methods. Quantitative methods, such as surveys,

Box 2.

Using SenseMaker to understand underlying structures and mental models

CRS conducted a gender analysis in Niger where it is implementing a program with two aims: (1) to stabilize and diversify livelihoods for improved food and nutrition security, and (2) to promote women and youth empowerment. This SenseMaker study (Johnson et. al, 2020) confirmed gender-based norms and behaviors identified during program design, such as internalized norms around male-dominated decision-making, coupled with women's submission that is linked to intimate partner violence. It also revealed links between girls' education and child marriage.

The study helped program staff understand some underlying structures and mental models that support gender-based norms and behaviors. For example, it showed that patriarchal gender norms have been internalized by women and girls and, to a lesser extent, by influencers (religious and community leaders, adult men, female heads of households). In the stories that were shared, almost half of women and girls acted on the basis of the belief that a man has a right to correct his wife and children, and that it is a woman's responsibility to make the marriage work. Well over half (58 percent) of the stories indicated that women's submissiveness was relevant to the story shared. The vast majority of women and girls indicated high levels of personal agreement with these beliefs.

Women and girls were found to be driven mostly by the fear of losing their social status, followed closely by fear of damaging family honor, and to a much lesser extent by fear of exclusion from communities. This showed the extent to which male-dominated belief systems were internalized by women and girls. These mental models mean women see men as responsible for providing for all households needs, which was cited as the cause of many cases of divorce, conflict, and marital violence. Although most women undertake activities to improve family food security and income, this is out of necessity as their husbands are unable to cover the families' needs, and not necessarily because they see this as desirable.

These insights gave CRS the basis for designing a social behavioral change strategy to address gender-based norms and behaviors that might otherwise have hindered achieving the goals of the program in Niger.

are useful for identifying the symptoms and trends of a situation, and to some extent explanatory patterns. Conventional qualitative methods are better suited to understand the underlying structures and mental models that explain events but have significant limitations. They rarely use a sufficiently large sample to give confidence that any findings cover the diversity of voices from key interest groups. They rarely involve a representative sample of a population, hindering generalizability of findings. More importantly, analysis of qualitative data relies heavily on interpretation by the researchers or evaluators of the information provided by respondents, making them intermediaries between respondents and information users.

What SenseMaker is and How it Works

SenseMaker is a complexity-aware, narrative-based method that can be used to conduct assessments, monitoring, evaluations (whether baseline, midterm, or final), and research studies. SenseMaker is based on narratives that respondents share and to which they give additional meaning. It recognizes that personal narratives—

Box 3.

Identifying unknown unknowns with SenseMaker

CRS conducted a resilience assessment in the Democratic Republic of the Congo in order to improve its program, which aims to achieve sustained nutrition, food security, and economic well-being (Gottret et. al, 2019). The assessment used SenseMaker to identify emerging practices that the program could scale. The stories showed that 41 percent of project participants considered that armed conflict— whether caused by social, ethnic, or religious differences—and, to a lesser extent, insecurity, theft, and domestic violence were the most important shocks or stressors they faced. The effects of these on emotional wellbeing, physical health, and social relations were evident in the narratives as well.

These experiences of armed conflict and domestic violence led to deteriorating individual behaviors, such as criminal behavior (theft, corruption, bribery), and an erosion of values, feeding dishonesty, nepotism, hate and envy, and creating serious obstacles to transformational change. It thus became obvious that the root causes of violence and conflict needed addressing, if the program was to have any sustained impact.

These unexpected findings highlighted the need for CRS to invest in peacebuilding, in addition to existing activities on nutrition, food security, and economic well-being, in order to build long-term resilience. This led the organization to leverage additional resources to implement its Binding, Bonding and Bridging (A3B) peacebuilding approach, including activities for individual self-transformation and trauma healing, bonding activities to strengthen relationships and mutual understanding within different identity groups, and bridging activities to develop trust among identity groups in order to foster dialogue in conflict resolution.

short accounts of people's experiences—allow better insights that can help contextualize knowledge.

The method involves gathering and analyzing many short, focused experiences from people. This shifts significant power of interpretation to the respondent and away from the researcher or evaluator. It has been specifically developed to better understand reality through respondents' eyes. Nuanced insights into their experiences can be revealed through visual data pattern analysis, statistical analysis, and textual analysis. SenseMaker can be used as a stand-alone method or in combination with other more conventional assessment, monitoring, evaluation, and research techniques. SenseMaker lends itself well to participatory practice. This guide provides many ideas on how to facilitate multi-stakeholder design and analysis.

Key Features of SenseMaker

SenseMaker has powerful features that, as a set, distinguish it from other methods of inquiry.

It uses a narrative as the entry point

The starting point is a narrative that the respondent chooses to share about a specific and lived experience, moment, or event that reveals what is important to them (see Box 4).

The SenseMaker method was developed based on the recognition that people make sense of the world around them through stories about their experiences. The starting point for the method is, therefore, the narratives that people share about a specific experience related to the topic of inquiry.

These short stories are usually about people's personal experiences. They are snippets about what is taking place and what is important for the person sharing

---

Box 4. Example of a SenseMaker narrative (original title and text as submitted)

The wrong initiative

"Last year my eldest son decided to go on an exodus, and he had no money. I was obliged to sell my cart including the cow to give him pocket money and to pay for his transportation. Today it has been exactly one year, and I don't know anything about him, nor has he sent me anything. Before his departure I was doing my business with the cart and I didn't want him to go, but as his father had the last word, he ordered me to let him go. Today I have no right to complain. I am worried if he would ever come back even if he didn't come with any money, I must not lose my eldest son and the cart both at the same time."

Adult woman, 31 years or older, Niger

that experience. This makes SenseMaker a powerful way to hear directly from the people closest to the issues, revealing the world through their eyes. Thus, depending on the purpose of the SenseMaker process, narratives can give voice to vulnerable people who have not been heard.

Narratives are triggered by a predesigned, open-ended question called the 'prompter'. The narratives can be shared in any language. They are documented in written form or through audio recordings. They can be submitted by the respondent or collected by a facilitator.

The prompter is intended to enable respondents to share factual experiences that are important to them, rather than to generate evaluative statements or opinions. The narrative is not a lengthy account of the experience, but rather a selective and focused account of what happened.

Since narratives provide an essential entry point to understanding more about a respondent's experience, the design and testing of the prompter is an important step that requires thoughtful testing and revision. A good prompter finds a balance between being broad enough to allow respondents to choose what is important to them, while being bounded enough so that the shared narratives focus on the study theme. Narratives may be shorter or longer, depending on the type of study and

Figure 1. Self-signification process using the body, pen & paper, or a tablet

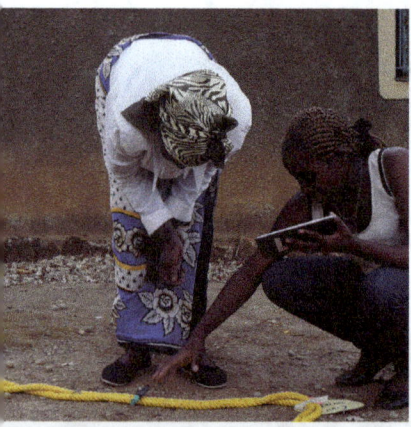
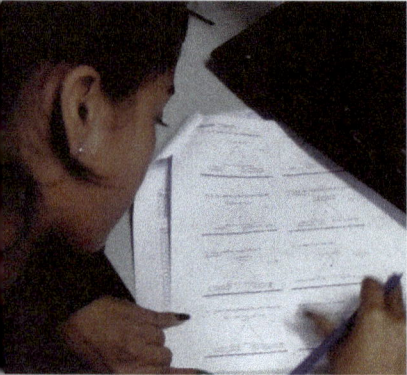

the planned use of the findings. For example, if the aim is to periodically monitor changes, a short narrative may be sufficient. On the other hand, if the aim is to conduct a more in-depth evaluation or to use the findings for advocacy, investing in generating more elaborate narratives might be considered.

It facilitates self-interpretation of experiences

Once a respondent has shared their experience, they are asked follow-up questions called 'signifier questions' that facilitate further reflection and interpretation on the experience. This self-signification process reduces the interpretive influence of the external evaluator or researcher during the analysis, and it provides additional layers of information about the experience shared by the respondent.

The narrative provides only a partial account of an experience. After the respondent has shared their narrative, predesigned follow-up questions prompt them to provide additional information and insights about their experience. These are called signifier questions, four types of which are specific to SenseMaker (core SenseMaker questions). The word 'signifier' comes from the self-signification process, in which respondents give meaning to the experience they share (Figure 1). In so doing, they provide a primary interpretation of their stories, which become that 'self-signified narratives'. This process reduces the interpretation bias of facilitators, evaluators, and researchers.

Self-signification is an essential step in the SenseMaker method, one that makes the design and testing of signifier questions as important as the design of the initial prompter. An instrument containing the prompter, a set of signifier questions, a set of multiple-choice questions (MCQs) about the sociodemographic characteristic of the respondent, and a set of collection protocol questions is called a signification framework.

It encourages respondents to deliberate over and nuance their responses

The way respondents are asked to provide their answers encourages nuanced and deliberative responses. The nature of the questions requires respondents to think before answering, encouraging them to take the time to reflect before giving a response, which is less common in conventional surveys. Questions are explicitly designed to reduce the potential for respondents to give socially desirable or gamed responses. Four types of signifier questions are core to the SenseMaker method: sliders, sliders with stones, triads, and canvases with stones.

The design process values ambiguity as a means of minimizing socially desirable answers—where respondents seek to respond in a way that they think will influence a project's design or implementation. This is particularly important when conducting an assessment or baseline evaluation that will be used in the design of an intervention, or to make decisions regarding primary project participants and implementation processes. Figure 2 shows a slider signifier question to which a respondent provides a nuanced answer between two extremes.

A Practical Guide for Using SenseMaker

It allows inclusion of many voices at scale and listening to differences

Unlike other qualitative methods, SenseMaker allows the inclusion of many voices—hundreds and sometimes thousands. A large number of narratives are captured, making it possible to listen to diverse perspectives on the same issue. The software helps disaggregate data to compare subgroups and, when robust sampling strategies are used, enables the use of statistical tests and allows inferences to be made.

Valuing each person's experience means there is no biased selection of 'best' stories or champion examples. With SenseMaker, all voices count—whether it is the voice of a project participant or a non-participant, whether it is a woman, man, youth, elder, or someone better off or worse off. In addition, if rigorous statistical sampling techniques are used, a sufficiently large sample will be collected, meaning the sampled voices will be representative of the population. This allows for statistical comparisons between different groups of respondents.

SenseMaker can also include the voices of stakeholders other than project participants—including implementing partners, government agencies, the private sector, and consumers. This provides a powerful way to compare multiple perspectives (Figure 3). This captures the perception of girls' behavior in the stories, illustrating the difference between stories told by fathers and those told by mothers (girls' empowerment project, Rwanda). Seeing the differences and similarities between stakeholders can help trigger ideas for action. Where there are an insufficient number of respondents in certain stakeholder groups, these stakeholders can still be engaged in collective interpretation processes during the sensemaking phase.

It empowers respondents as they reflect on their experiences

When facilitated properly, SenseMaker has the potential to raise awareness among respondents, empowering them through selecting, sharing, and making sense of their experiences.

Figure 2. Slider signifier question enabling nuanced answer between two extremes

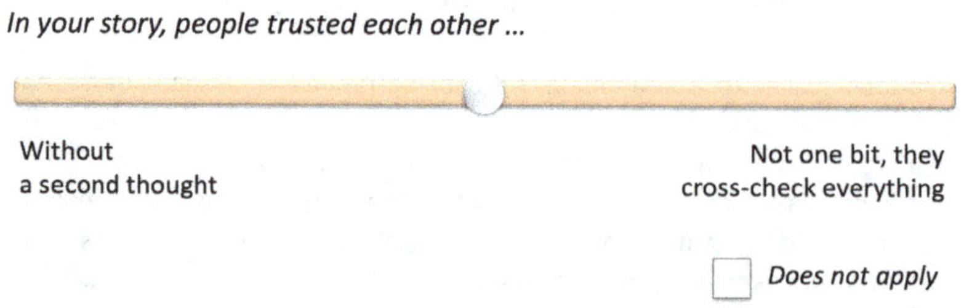

In your story, people trusted each other ...

Without a second thought

Not one bit, they cross-check everything

☐ *Does not apply*

During many SenseMaker studies, the respondents were systematically asked how they felt while sharing and signifying their experiences. It showed that SenseMaker made it easier for respondents with varying levels of literacy to participate. It helped them to reflect on the experiences they shared in a way that created an awareness of their assets and capabilities, as well as their achievements. Their reflections generated lessons that they indicated would be useful in similar situations in future. In one study with refugees (Gottret and Kast 2018), the facilitators asked respondents exit questions after the interview. They found that respondents appreciated and enjoyed the process of responding. It helped them, they said, to reflect on their lived experience in a different way. Some respondents said that this was the first time they had talked about what had happened to them. Others said that they appreciated the opportunity to be heard.

SenseMaker can be of value to respondents as they share and reflect on the experiences that are important to them. It can give them an opportunity to come up with ideas and solutions to pursue better outcomes. When sensemaking includes collective interpretation events, powerful insights are generated for the stakeholders involved—not only those who commissioned the SenseMaker process.

It values weak signals as important to adaptive management

A SenseMaker analysis can easily reveal dominant patterns and tease out means and medians in the data. But it also values individual experiences and weak signals or outliers. Weak signals can help to identify aspects of a situation that can provide opportunities for innovation or support to reach positive outcomes (emergent practices). Such signals can also point to challenges or problems that

Figure 3. Signifier question comparing several people's perspectives

could be addressed or reduced. This feature is fundamental in supporting adaptive management.

The analytical process involves flipping agilely between individual stories and the larger patterns of which they are part. All stories are analyzed, not only for averages, but also to detect unusual patterns and to compare differing perspectives and views. Just as conventional MEAL and research methods can generate statistics from quantitative data, SenseMaker allows statistical analysis. This analytical process identifies positive and negative outliers, called weak signals, as indicators of emerging opportunities or concerns that merit further investment (emergent practices) or that might need addressing (threats). This is essential if monitoring and evaluation (M&E) is to support collaboration, learning, and adaptation.

For example, Rikolto International (previously Veco) developed a one-week sensemaking process, during which farmers and other value-chain stakeholders engaged in discussions on what might be needed to increase positive patterns or to reduce problematic ones. These discussions aimed to support decision-making and follow-up actions that nudged progress toward a desired goal.

CRS has also been developing a SenseMaker-based tool for assessing how far farmers have advanced along pathways to prosperity and their resilience to shocks and stressors (Gottret 2017). From start to finish, this type of evaluation can take two months, allowing teams to make decisions and take action for better quality implementation and performance. This ability to support programs in operating effectively in complex contexts is a fundamental characteristic of SenseMaker, making it a valuable complexity-aware tool for designing, implementing, monitoring, and evaluating any initiative.

Figure 4. Signifier question (triad) giving wider relevance of a single story ('controlling the damage' cluster) (peacebuilding project in Mindanao, Philippines)

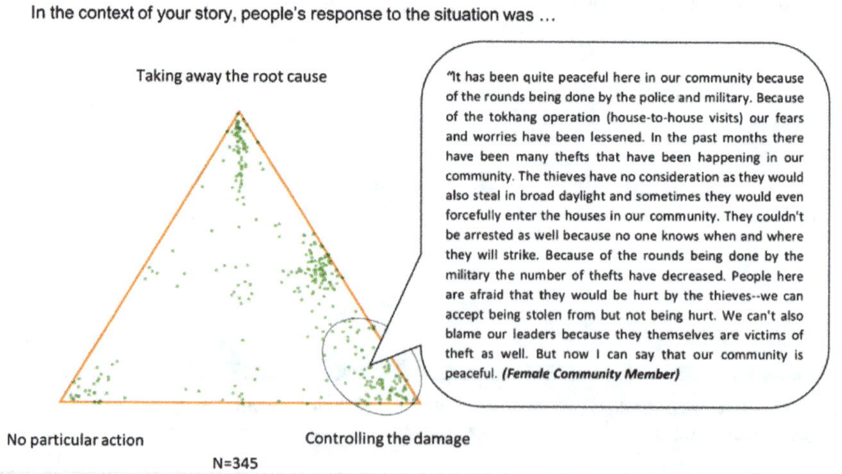

In the context of your story, people's response to the situation was ...

Taking away the root cause

No particular action   Controlling the damage
                    N=345

"It has been quite peaceful here in our community because of the rounds being done by the police and military. Because of the tokhang operation (house-to-house visits) our fears and worries have been lessened. In the past months there have been many thefts that have been happening in our community. The thieves have no consideration as they would also steal in broad daylight and sometimes they would even forcefully enter the houses in our community. They couldn't be arrested as well because no one knows when and where they will strike. Because of the rounds being done by the military the number of thefts have decreased. People here are afraid that they would be hurt by the thieves--we can accept being stolen from but not being hurt. We can't also blame our leaders because they themselves are victims of theft as well. But now I can say that our community is peaceful. *(Female Community Member)*

It combines qualitative and quantitative data through analysis of visual patterns, text, and statistical data

Qualitative and quantitative data are analyzed together to complement each other and produce better insights. The SenseMaker approach allows for an agile analytical process that combines the visualization of patterns from multiple responses, the selection of narratives from dominant and weak patterns for text analysis, and the combination of responses to visualize association or correlation. Strong patterns with large visual clusters of responses can be spotted quickly, as can outliers, with direct access to the underlying narratives to further enhance interpretation and contextualization of the observed patterns.

As soon as responses are uploaded, immediate visualization, observation, and exploration of emerging response patterns is possible. Once patterns of interest have been identified, specific stories related to each pattern can be read and used to assist in interpretation and contextualization. People's voices in stories can be linked to quantitative patterns that can shed light on the wider relevance of an individual story (Figures 4 and 5). By visualizing patterns across a set of narratives and reading the associated narratives, a more open-ended, surprise-seeking analysis is made possible, and premature conclusions are avoided. Signifiers can be combined with each other or with other question types to filter the stories into smaller clusters, or subgroups, to detect differences among groups of respondents, as well as dominant patterns or outliers. Analysis can also include a more structured, assumption-testing phase of looking at visual patterns, narratives, and statistics, though this usually occurs once the more exploratory approach to analysis has been taken. Such more comprehensive analysis involves analyzing and visualizing data using various software, from the more basic (such as Microsoft Excel) to the more sophisticated (Tableau, PowerBI, R, Stata, SPSS).

Figure 5. Signifier question (triad) highlighting a minor story cluster ('no particular action' cluster) (peacebuilding project in Mindanao, Philippines)

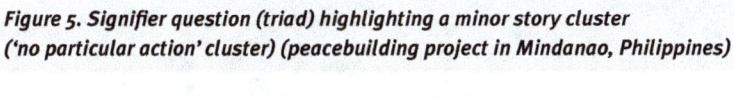

In the context of your story, people's response to the situation was …

"I was at home yesterday when I heard shooting outside. There were two separate shots and it was around 11:00 at night. I was shocked when it happened, because someone has died again. Every week there is such an incident, and so I am quite used to it. I don't know what the cause of the shooting was. The next day I found out from my neighbor that the one who died was just renting here and just got involved in a conflict between drug addicts. She was mistaken for an asset of the police so she was killed. That is how it is in our community; when there is a new face s/he is always looked at as a police asset. No one reported this to the police and no one came to the aid of the victim. People here are used to keeping things to themselves, because we are afraid that we would get involved and be killed."
(Female Youth Leader)

Taking away the root cause

No particular action   N=345   Controlling the damage

It reframes indicators of success

Analysis using SenseMaker can provide a complementary way to frame indicators of success in terms of the desirability of certain kinds of narratives and visual patterns. Targets can be identified by making statements such as: 'Through the program, we would like to see more stories or responses like this ..., and fewer like that.'

Conventional MEAL methods and processes often rely on selecting specific indicators of progress, which are the basis of targets for the intervention. Analysis focuses on confirming or refuting progress towards these targets. While conventional methods may also seek explanations for why efforts have been effective or not, finding the answers to such questions can be problematic. The findings that SenseMaker reveals can provide an additional way to frame indicators and targets: in terms of the desirability of narratives and response patterns. For example, targets may be identified like this: 'Through the program, we would like more stories like this ... and fewer like that .... ?' Some organizations have begun to use the key signifier questions as alternative indicators for monitoring and reporting program progress. The example in Figure 6 shows a triad used for the baseline of the A3B peacebuilding program implemented by CRS in the Philippines. Through its interventions, the program aims to build the capacity of local communities and local peace and order structures to deal with conflict. Over the life of the program, it aims to see more stories in which these groups are perceived as being able to solve the problem (lower part of the graph).

Figure 6. Signifier question (triad) indicating the desired pattern during the program's lifespan

What is required to solve the conflict situation in your story?

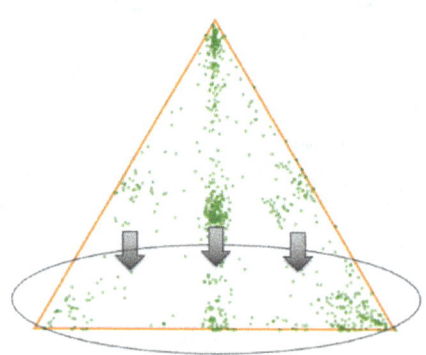

All stories (N=810)

The SenseMaker Process

The SenseMaker process has four phases: preparation, design, collection, and sensemaking (Figure 7). These form the basis of the structure of this guide. Although the phases are presented sequentially, the SenseMaker process unfolds iteratively. Each phase involves a set of activities that need to be covered sooner or later. The purpose, context, and organizational conditions lead to unique SenseMaker processes. The activities listed below provide an overview of what is involved in each phase to help ensure the basics are being covered, and that good practices are built up through experience. These are illustrated by the cases on which the guide draws.

The four phases of the SenseMaker process are briefly described below, with detailed guidance found in the following chapters:
- Phase 1: Preparation
- Phase 2: Design
- Phase 3: Collection
- Phase 4: Sensemaking

Deciding to use SenseMaker

Before diving into SenseMaker, it is important to determine whether the method is suited to the intended purpose and if it is to be used alongside other methods or on its own. As SenseMaker is still relatively unknown, those making the decision can benefit from a solid introduction to the method. This will help understand its potential and limitations, clarify how findings are presented, and show how it can contribute to the intended purpose. This information is essential to make an informed decision.

Figure 7. Phases of a SenseMaker process

Phase 1: Preparation	Phase 2: Design	Phase 3: Collection	Phase 4: Sensemaking
• Establish core team • Finalize purpose • Design process • Prepare budget • Secure support from leadership • Think through ethics from design to use • Make detailed plan	• Develop analytical framing • Design sampling strategy • Draft signification framework • Test, revise, translate framework • Create digital version of framework	• Prepare for data collection • Train facilitators • Conduct final user test and revise framework • Facilitate collection • Monitor collection and data quality	• Prepare for analysis • Decide on sensemaking strategy • Conduct primary analysis • Conduct collective interpretation • Conduct comprehensive analysis • Communicate and use findings

Phase 1: Preparation for the SenseMaker process

Once the decision has been made to use SenseMaker, the Preparation phase begins by laying a solid foundation for an effective SenseMaker process. This phase needs to be documented in a SenseMaker process plan, or Scope of Work, that is agreed on by all interested parties.

Planning and agreeing on the SenseMaker process. Once the green light has been given, the process needs careful preparation: clarifying the purpose; clarifying complementarity with other methods being used; specifying hardware and software needs; creating a team with clear roles and responsibilities; developing a timeline and budget; and agreeing on leadership, team coordination, and communication. Agreements about the why, what, who, how, and when form the basis of a SenseMaker process plan. Discussing and signing off on the plan can lay the foundation for a smooth process.

Securing support from leadership. In addition to an allocated budget, a quality SenseMaker process requires a core team tasked with overseeing the process from start to finish; the contribution of thematic experts during the Design and Sensemaking phases, as needed; the coordination of logistics during the Collection phase; and active participation of program staff, partners, and project participants for collective interpretation during the Sensemaking phase. All this requires the support and commitment of the organization's leadership.

Phase 2: Design of the signification framework

A good design is fundamental for high-quality findings and optimal use; it lays the foundation for the rest of the process. The design process requires sufficient time, enough knowledgeable contributors, and good facilitation. This phase merges into the Collection phase through testing and revising the signification framework. With a clear purpose and focus agreed upon during the Preparation phase, the design process begins by identifying the voices and perspectives that need to be heard but are often not attended to sufficiently. The groups and subgroups of interest can then be mapped to review and revise the sampling and stratification strategy, as needed.

Defining the analytical framing. To ensure a focused and high-quality design, an analytical framing is essential. This can be selected from existing frameworks or may be developed specifically for this purpose. This step may require a focused literature review and consultation with thematic experts, as well as input from people with hands-on experience of the topic of inquiry, whether as practitioners or as intended participants of an intervention.

Drafting the signification framework. This differs considerably from designing traditional surveys or interview guides. A well-formulated prompter is crucial to obtain narratives that can reveal insights about the topic of interest. The learning questions, key concepts, and analytical framing developed during the Preparation phase lay the groundwork for a good design that addresses the learning or research questions. These are used to draft follow-up questions that also require careful design.

Testing the signification framework. The full draft of the framework is always tested, whether or not the SenseMaker process requires the creation of a new framework, or the adaption or replication of an existing one. This step includes preliminary and in situ testing by those designing the framework, and user testing by the people who will conduct the interviews. Testing usually starts with a paper version of the signification framework and if collection is to be digital, testing with the digital version is needed to check all aspects are working well. This can be part of the user testing phase during the facilitator training.

Configuring the digital version of the signification framework. The digital version of the framework is configured in Designer to allow data entry through a browser or an app.

Phase 3: Collection of narratives and facilitation of their self-signification

Based on our experience, the Collection phase involves facilitators engaging with respondents for meaningful conversation. There are cases where there is no need for facilitators as respondents can share their narratives and self-signify it by themselves, but these are very rare in applications focused on development practice, humanitarian response and social justice work.

The facilitators prompt respondents to share their narratives about the experiences they feel are significant, which results in qualitative (textual) data. They then facilitate the respondents' self-signification using follow-up signifier questions. This results in quantitative (numerical) data. Good facilitation during the collection process is essential to ensure high-quality data, as this lays the foundation for good analysis and robust findings.

Preparing for collection. An effective and high-quality collection process requires thorough preparation. This includes the selection of the facilitators. If external facilitators are being used, they need to be contracted. A collection plan is drawn up to guide how facilitators are to be distributed, and includes a calendar of activities, as well as listing the logistics and support needed. Facilitator kits that include the collection devices (tablets or smartphones), paper copies of the signification framework, and all materials for the facilitation processes are prepared in advance.

Training facilitators and conducting a final user testing. The facilitators are critical to the quality of the SenseMaker process, which involves much more than simply filling in a survey. The facilitators undertake the fundamental task of collecting the narratives and supporting the respondents in signifying their experiences. Investing in high-quality and thorough hands-on training of facilitators is well worth the effort.

Facilitators need to be trained in the basic SenseMaker method, to understand each question in the signification framework, to know how to facilitate each type of signifier question, to be able to create a rapport with respondents so as to encourage sharing and reflection, and to ensure that the collection process is ethical. During training, facilitators help conduct a final test of the signification framework to fine-tune the language and to ensure local appropriateness.

Facilitating the collection process. Facilitating the collection of the narratives and the self-signification process is at the core of the Collection phase. Facilitators follow the protocols that have been established, learned, and practiced during the training and final user testing. Facilitators need to ensure that the process is appropriate for the context and that collection is ethical.

Monitoring collection to ensure quality. The first days of collection offer an opportunity to finesse the practice, so accompanying the team of facilitators is important. Such in-person monitoring during the first days needs to be planned in advance. Quality checks of the uploaded narratives and responses to the signifier questions can help identify and solve problems with individual facilitation and technology, as they emerge.

Phase 4: Sensemaking with stakeholders

Sensemaking involves visualizing, examining, and recombining the qualitative and quantitative data that SenseMaker generates. It then involves analyzing and interpreting the collected narratives and data with different stakeholders, triggering individual and collective reflections that offer new insights. These then inform decisions for programming, advocacy, or local action. This is a multistage process, with much iteration between visualizing patterns, and an open-ended and structured analysis.

Preparing for sensemaking. After the collection process has finished, the dataset is cleaned and prepared for analysis. This may involve removing duplicate narratives or other errors, recategorizing or retrospectively categorizing responses, introducing translated narratives, or replacing narratives that have too many typing or grammatical errors. Once the data are cleaned, access to the dataset can be given to those involved in analysis.

Primary analysis. The first step in an initial exploratory analysis is to ensure the SenseMaker core team members have been trained in the use of its analytical and visualization capabilities. The analysis team then carries out a primary analysis by looking at visual patterns for all signifier questions, reading the narratives, and characterizing respondents using MCQs designed for this purpose. Findings are discussed and form the basis of a plan for further analysis and documentation. The learning questions and the analytical framing will inform and help focus the sensemaking process. Based on this, collective interpretation workshops with the SenseMaker process stakeholders can be planned and prepared.

Collective interpretation. Different types of events (remote and/or face-to-face) can be held with the SenseMaker process stakeholders, as per available resources and time. These may include intended project participants; facilitators; implementing partners; program, MEAL and management staff; peer organizations; other key stakeholders; and donors. At these events, primary analysis findings are shared, and additional interpretation is undertaken. New avenues for analysis can emerge and ideas are generated for action. These may include adjusting the implementation strategies and operational plans of existing projects to provide adaptive management, or to feed into the design of future initiatives.

Comprehensive analysis. Comprehensive analysis can be used to further explore the data in order to respond to specific learning questions, or components or concepts in the analytical framework. It can also be used to respond to questions that emerge during primary analysis or collective interpretation. Comprehensive analysis requires a more structured (focused or guided) approach than primary analysis, and usually requires the time and input of people with specific quantitative and qualitative analysis skills.

Communication and use. This guidance does not aim to provide comprehensive advice on communication and the use of findings, but it does aim to ensure that the SenseMaker process is user-focused. For this purpose, it is important to revisit the stakeholder analysis conducted during the Preparation phase, in order to develop user-targeted, customized communication products to engage key stakeholders and to share findings, analysis, and recommendations with them. This will ensure that, after several interactions of analysis, interpretation, and documentation, different communication products can be developed on the basis of stakeholder analysis.

The Software

A SenseMaker process requires: (a) a software license for the organization or project, and (b) software to configure signification frameworks, collect, access, analyze, and visualize data. Licenses can be purchased directly from The Cynefin Company, the company that has developed SenseMaker. Cost options need to be discussed with a SenseMaker professional or directly with The Cynefin Company.

At the time this guide went into press, the proprietary Cynefin Company software SenseMaker Suite offered design, analyze, dashboard and data export functions, all accessible via a personalized login. Users can digitally configure signification frameworks, collect data via a browser and an app, store data online, perform basic Master dataset manipulation, visualize and summarize data, and export data from the server.

It is common to use third party visualization and analytical software, including Excel, R, Stata, SPSS, and Tableau. Using third party software to digitally configure a signification framework and for data entry is possible, if less common. It requires a good understanding of the methodology, question types, data structure, and needs to be discussed directly with The Cynefin Company.

Suitability Assessment

31 **Comparing SenseMaker to Common Methods of Inquiry**

34 **Becoming Acquainted with the SenseMaker Method**

37 **Criteria to Assess the Suitability of SenseMaker**

SenseMaker is sufficiently different from conventional methods to warrant investing time in understanding how it works and what it can and cannot do, so an informed decision can be made.

Suitability Assessment

Like any method, SenseMaker is not appropriate for all contexts, purposes, and information needs. Deciding whether to use this method requires clarity about its appropriateness to the task at hand and to the operating conditions.
Making an informed decision will help align expectations with what SenseMaker can and cannot do.

To make an informed decision, the team will need:

- a basic understanding of the method, its underlying principles, how it differs from other methods, and the process involved;
- clarity on the purpose of the study and on the type of information and insights needed to serve that purpose;
- access to experienced SenseMaker practitioners or a well-planned capacity building process; and
- realistic expectations about the human and financial resources needed, and the time the SenseMaker process will take from start to finish.

Comparing SenseMaker to Common Methods of Inquiry

SenseMaker is a relatively new method in social change initiatives, development projects and humanitarian response. It is sufficiently different from conventional methods to warrant investing time in understanding how it works and what it can and cannot do. To start making an informed decision on whether to use SenseMaker, it is helpful to set up a team to assess suitability and feasibility, and to involve a skilled SenseMaker practitioner. To make an informed decision, people will need a basic understanding of what the method is, how it works, and (importantly) how it compares to other quantitative and qualitative methods they might be familiar with. They should also understand how it can complement more conventional methods (Table 1).

Table 1. Comparing SenseMaker with other methods of inquiry

	QUANTITATIVE METHODS	QUALITATIVE METHODS
Information	Changes in predefined variables in a specific context, and differences between predefined cohorts and over time.	In-depth experiences that describe and explain a situation or change process, the factors that influenced the process, and the outcomes.
Focus	Comparing specific interventions and anticipated observable change variables that can be disaggregated by cohorts. Allows before–after and with–without comparisons.	Understanding change processes, the context in which they take place, the factors that contributed to the processes, the outcomes, and the value of the processes.
Type/data	Numerical and categorical data.	Textual data that may require coding, expert analysis, interpretation, and quantitative text analysis.
Analytical approach	Descriptive and inferential statistical analysis, with a focus on means, medians, and standard deviations, aimed at assessing the spread of responses from the correlations and cause–effect relations. The analysis aims to generate insights and conclusions that are representative of the study population and to test for statistically significant differences between different subgroups of that population. Visualizations based on analytical outputs are also produced.	Deductive or inductive qualitative data analysis, with a focus on a thorough examination of the themes of study, in order to better understand social processes and the multiple factors that influence them. The analysis aims to obtain valid insights and conclusions. Visualizations based on analytical outputs are also produced.
Main type of reasoning[1]	**Deductive:** If the premises are all true, then the conclusion must be true. This begins with the assertion of a general rule, and then proceeds to a confirmed specific conclusion, using statistical tests to generalize sample findings to the overall population.	**Inductive:** If the premises are all true, then the conclusion is probably true. This begins with observations that are specific and limited in scope, and then proceeds to valid generalized conclusions. This approach is used when little is known about the phenomena being studied.

1. *Reasoning is the process of using existing knowledge to draw conclusions, make predictions, or construct explanations.*

SENSEMAKER

Information

Respondents' experiences of a situation or change process, and their own coding of those experiences, which reduces the influence of external interpretation. This self-signification process can reveal information on the influences of different factors, such as behaviors and values, access to assets, strategies employed, actions taken and outcomes. This allows multiple combinations of responses to dig deeper in order to understand (layers of) causes.

Focus

Includes both options for qualitative and quantitative approaches. Understanding change processes, the context in which they take place, the factors that contribute to them, and their outcomes and values, on the basis of respondents' narratives and self-signification. It also allows before-after and with-without comparisons, if the process and sampling have been designed with these in mind.

Type/data

Qualitative textual data that is interpreted by the respondent, generating quantitative numerical data.

Analytical approach

Descriptive and inferential statistical analysis and deductive or inductive qualitative data analysis, with some limitations inherent in the method.[2]

Visualizations form the basis of analysis and collective interpretation and are available immediately. Analysis can include means, medians, and standard deviations, and pays attention to outliers (known as 'weak signals') as potentially important indicators of opportunities and problems.

Main type of reasoning

Abductive or hypothesis-generating: Often referred to as a variation of inductive reasoning, this begins with an incomplete set of observations and proceeds to the likeliest possible explanation for the set. Abductive reasoning yields the kind of information needed for daily decision-making, which tries its best with the (often incomplete) information at hand (Thagard and Cameron 1997).

---

2. For example, narratives may be short, and are very likely to not contain all the information about the experience, which is instead captured by follow-up questions. This may limit the scope of qualitative analysis. The quantitative data captured through some core SenseMaker signifier questions is relative, rather than absolute; this affects the approach to statistical analysis (if required).

Becoming Acquainted with the SenseMaker Method

There are several ways to gain a basic understanding of the SenseMaker method:

- Explore existing SenseMaker publications, such as case studies, articles, reports, and blog posts. This guide offers an introduction to SenseMaker, a broad range of examples from different processes and topics (see below), and references to case studies.
- Attend an introductory training session conducted by a skilled SenseMaker practitioner who can help to assess the use and applicability of the method for one's project or initiative.
- Consult colleagues who have used SenseMaker in similar organizations and contexts—and ideally for similar topics.

Uses of SenseMaker

SenseMaker has been used in a variety of ways and contexts. Table 2 provides some examples of SenseMaker studies conducted for different purposes: assessments, baseline studies, monitoring, and evaluation.

Table 2. Examples of SenseMaker studies

Assessments and appraisals

The Inclusive Business Scan assessed and generated insights about the inclusivity of business models within smallholder supply chains. The aim is to adjust value-chain support interventions, provide feedback to buyers and farmer organizations, and stimulate dialogue among value-chain actors. The generic SenseMaker framework can be used in different value chains with minor adaptations, which reduces design and analysis time and cost.

Application: Rikolto International (previously VECO). Between 2012 and 2016 in Indonesia, Senegal, Nicaragua, Ecuador, and the Democratic Republic of the Congo (DRC). For more information, see: The Inclusive Business Scan.

Resilience assessment: After trying several approaches to assess resilience and evaluate progress toward building resilience capabilities—with mixed results—CRS decided to use the SenseMaker method to develop a tool for this purpose, and tested it interactively in nine case studies in Latin America, Southeast Asia, and East Africa (2016-2017), as well as in the DRC (2017–2018). Throughout the different applications, the design was further adapted and refined.

Application: CRS, Guatemala, Nicaragua, Indonesia, Bangladesh, East Timor, Tanzania, Kenya, Uganda, DRC (2016–2018). For more information, see Understanding and assessing resilience (Gottret 2017).

4,000 Voices, a national representative study on attitudes towards adolescent girls to focus a girls' empowerment program, generate baseline data for assessing program impact, and inform policy design. A parallel effort in Ethiopia collected 4,800 stories.

Application: Girl Effect, Rwanda and Ethiopia (2013/2014).

The **A3B Peace project baseline** aimed to understand how people perceive the effect of peace and conflict situations on relationships, the level of trust, and their feelings of safety in their communities. It also generated a baseline for the project.

Application: CRS, Philippines (2016–2017).

Partnership and capacity strengthening tool (pcsSCAN), a real-time collection and visualization (PowerBI dashboard) of feedback on capacity strengthening across the entire organization. Capacity strengthening happens through online learning, face-to-face capacity building, coaching, and mentoring, as well as through accessing helpful tools, guides, studies, and other learning and practitioner resources. These resources are not static, requiring continuous adjustment to remain relevant and beneficial. pcsSCAN enables CRS to listen to staff and partners, and makes it easy to collect, interpret and act on their feedback (CRS 2018).

Application: CRS, globally (since 2017).

Review of a multisectoral orphans and vulnerable children (OVC) program: This assessed the hypothesized relationships and explicit assumptions identified in the project's theory of change. It was part of a wide-ranging midterm review of a multisectoral OVC program funded by the President's Emergency Plan for AIDS Relief (PEPFAR). Other methods included a large-scale cross-sectional survey, key informant interviews, and focus group discussions. A SenseMaker process was conducted in a sub-sample of households (n = 480) from the household survey. This design allowed the survey and SenseMaker data to be exported, merged, and analyzed in a statistical analysis package (Tangible benefits to child wellbeing seen among households participating in Savings and Internal Lending Communities (SILC), CRS 2018).

Application: CRS, Nigeria (2016).

Making sense of refugee support: CRS used SenseMaker for the final evaluation of a nine-year program supporting Colombian refugees, Venezuelan migrants, and vulnerable Ecuadorians. CRS, with its implementing partner the Missionaries of St. Charles Borromeo, chose the method because many participants had undergone traumatic experiences, and CRS wanted to minimize the risk of causing further trauma. The respondents indicated that they appreciated the process of responding and being listened to; it helped them reflect on their experiences. Some said it was the first time they had talked about what had happened to them. SenseMaker enabled the evaluation team to remain people-centered (Making sense of refugee support: using narratives to evaluate a program to protect and integrate refugees in Ecuador, Gottret and Kast 2018).

Application: CRS, Colombia, Venezuela, Ecuador (2016–2018).

Evaluation of seventeen years of agriculture and livelihoods programming in Nicaragua. CRS used SenseMaker to assess and analyze farmer segmentation and livelihood-outcome dynamics, as well as the role of external intervention in promoting a 'pathway to prosperity' for farm families in Nicaragua (Gottret et al. 2017). This study not only generated much-needed evidence on the achievements and challenges of the program. It also produced important new insights into resilience, which led to a multi-country and regional resilience assessment, also using SenseMaker.

Application: CRS, Nicaragua (2015–2016).

The People on the Move assessment generated insights about displaced people's experiences and the power they had to make decisions. The studies sought to capture the agency of displaced residents and returnees of different ages and genders in the Central African Republic and Iraq. These studies inform Oxfam's work on refugees and displacement, which especially influences the displaced people's decisions and the scope they have for exerting their agency. The studies offer gender-differentiated and assumption-challenging insights into the experiences of displacement.

Application: Oxfam GB, Central African Republic and Kurdistan, Iraq (2017–2018). For more information Smith et al. (2018).

Formative research on nutrition-sensitive agriculture in Guatemala: CRS Guatemala conducted this research to better understand the underlying causes of chronic malnutrition in Guatemala's Western Highlands, with the aim of designing more effective projects to address this long-term challenge (Merchan, Gottret, and McQuillan 2018). This research provided important insights for future program design. The three key findings were: (1) poultry production holds significant potential to address nutritional and income needs of families; (2) while climate-stressed agroecosystems can have a significant negative impact on food security, climate impacts can be mitigated with climate-resilient water and soil practices; and (3) savings and loans are vital coping mechanisms for food security challenges and to build resilience.

Application: CRS, Guatemala (2017–2018).

Criteria to Assess the Suitability of SenseMaker

There are multiple criteria that can help assess whether SenseMaker is suitable.

- **Fitness for purpose:** Is SenseMaker an appropriate method for the purpose of the study, and will it provide the type of information needed for the assessment, monitoring, evaluation, or research?
- **Voices at scale:** Is there access to a sufficient number of respondents to draw conclusions or construct explanations with the required level of disaggregation (e.g. by gender, region, age)?
- **Stakeholder involvement:** Can sufficient involvement and participation of stakeholders and participants be ensured throughout the processes of design, collection, and sensemaking?
- **Organizational conditions:** Does the organization have the resources needed for a successful SenseMaker process: budget, staff time, staff capabilities, support from a skilled SenseMaker practitioner and leadership buy-in?

Teams can add other criteria to support the decision-making process, but these key criteria proved important in the projects listed in Table 2. Each of these criteria is discussed in detail in the following sections.

Fitness for purpose

SenseMaker is useful for understanding and assessing less tangible and less measurable aspects, issues, and changes.

SenseMaker generates visual patterns, quantitative data, and short narratives, and has the potential to reveal different views and perspectives, relationships, and interactions within the complex settings in which development practices operate. It is most appropriate when users wish to gain insights into less tangible and less measurable concepts, such as behavioral and cultural changes, values, gender, governance, trust, well-being, inclusion, social norms, resilience, and dignity. SenseMaker is not suitable for simply measuring quantitative indicators, such as production, costs, sales, income, child weight and height, or number of food groups.

The clearer the purpose and use of the study, the better decision-makers can understand what needs to be assessed. It is crucial that those involved in the decision are fully aware and have appropriate expectations of what type of data and insights SenseMaker generates, and what type it does not. It is highly recommended that first-time users involve experienced users to help them think through these issues.

Voices at scale

A sample should be large enough to generate desired insights, but small enough to keep the process economical.

An essential criterion for deciding on the use of SenseMaker is to understand whose voices are important for the topic of interest, how many can be captured, and whether resources and access are available. If it is necessary to collect narratives from a specific group, a decision needs to be made on how many can be collected, considering existing constraints and whether this sample size is sufficient to generate informative and actionable insights.

In practice, SenseMaker sample sizes can vary from a few dozen to a few thousand entries. However, if the sample is too small, it may not be worth investing in a SenseMaker process, as there will be limitations for analysis and disaggregation using data visualization. For example, if you are working with a self-help group of only twenty women, the main group from which you want to collect stories, the investment and effort involved in using SenseMaker will be too high for what it will give. Other methods, like semi-structured interviews, would be more appropriate and cost-effective. Nevertheless, SenseMaker has been successfully used in workshop environments with smaller samples, using its visualization and analysis tools.

Stakeholder involvement

SenseMaker works best when stakeholders are involved in participatory design and collective interpretation processes.

This guide promotes the implementation and use of SenseMaker as a participatory and collaborative process. The involvement and participation of stakeholders at different stages of the SenseMaker process enhances the quality, use, and effectiveness of the method, and ensures that it adds value beyond the collection process and reporting mode. Experience shows that this is particularly important during the Design and Sensemaking phases (Deprez and Guijt, 2021). The participation of various stakeholders in the collective design and interpretation processes fosters richer insights into the context, changes peoples' perspectives, stimulates debate and conversations, leads to a shared understanding of issues, challenges and possible solutions, and fosters collaborative action. Nevertheless, this also applies to other more conventional methods when being user-focused is a guiding principle.

Organizational conditions

A high-quality SenseMaker process requires an appropriate mix of human and financial resources, as well as leadership support.

Like any other method, SenseMaker requires an appropriate budget, sufficient staff time, the necessary competencies, and good managerial and logistical support. For first-time users, good technical support and advice is needed to ensure a quality process. Support from a skilled SenseMaker practitioner is thus strongly recommended. In addition, it is best if an on-site core group designs and implements the SenseMaker process from start to finish, with one of its members designated as the SenseMaker process lead. Experience shows that a realistic time frame needs to be agreed upon, and that leadership support is essential to successfully implement a SenseMaker process.

Making the decision to use SenseMaker

A helpful way to assess the suitability of SenseMaker is to review the considerations outlined above. Box 5 presents some of the questions that can assist potential SenseMaker users in making an informed decision about its suitability. The list has been used by SenseMaker practitioners as a guide for the predesign stage, or as a formal checklist to make the go/no-go decision. It is not exhaustive and can be complemented with other questions and criteria relevant to the context. By discussing and answering these questions, the team will generate information that is essential not only in deciding on the use of SenseMaker, but also in kickstarting the design of the process.

Box 5. Questions to ask before deciding to use SenseMaker

FITNESS FOR PURPOSE

- What is the purpose of the process?
- What are the main aspects, concepts, and changes to be assessed? How tangible and measurable are they?
- Would the type of information generated by SenseMaker respond to our information needs?

VOICES AT SCALE

- Whose voices are we interested in hearing?
- How do we want to disaggregate these voices to filter the analysis?
- What number of respondents, overall and in each subgroup of interest, is required for the process? Is this realistic?

STAKEHOLDER INVOLVEMENT

- Can we ensure sufficient internal staff and partner engagement during the design, collection, and sensemaking phases?
- Should we engage external stakeholders in the process? Where and when?

ORGANIZATIONAL CONDITIONS

- Can we secure the advice needed from an experienced SenseMaker practitioner to implement the SenseMaker process?
- Do we have an in-country core team that can allocate time to coordinate and support the process?
- Do we have the time and resources to develop in-country core team capacity, if needed?
- Do we have the financial resources to conduct the process from start to finish?
- Do we have a realistic time frame to get the work done?
- Do we have sufficient leadership support?

Phase 1: Preparation

- 41 **Core Decisions about the SenseMaker Process**
- 43 **Main Considerations**
- 49 **Ethical Considerations**
- 51 **Developing the SenseMaker Process Plan**

Taking the time to lay a solid foundation is essential for an effective SenseMaker process, and requires thinking through purpose, participation, and team composition.

Phase 1: Preparation

Once the decision to use SenseMaker has been made, it can be tempting to dive straight into the process by training the core team and designing the signification framework. However, experience has shown the importance of laying a solid foundation for an effective SenseMaker process. If this phase is undertaken in haste, or without giving serious thought to the key questions documented in the SenseMaker process plan, then the quality of the SenseMaker process might be undermined.

Core Decisions about the SenseMaker Process

There are three decisions that strongly determine the design and implementation of a SenseMaker process: purpose, participation, and team composition. Each of these decisions is a spectrum between two options, with the purpose of the study determining where along the spectrum the choice will land.

1. Core purpose

The purpose of the SenseMaker process is fully...

Results-oriented ———————————————— Process-oriented

A results-oriented approach focuses on using the results and insights generated from the SenseMaker study. In this scenario, the steps of the SenseMaker process are organized to make it as efficient as possible, without compromising robustness. By comparison, when process is prioritized, participation in the different stages is a learning and an empowering process for participants (Deprez and Guijt, 2021). Careful attention is therefore paid to who to involve, enabling their participation and ownership of the different stages of the process.

2. Extent of stakeholder participation

The SenseMaker process will involve a ....

Small core group ———————————————— Large group of stakeholders

The number and types of actors involved in a SenseMaker process will depend on the nature of the organization or initiative and the purpose of the study. A limited number of people are easier to manage, while having many stakeholders involved in the design, collection, and sensemaking will require more coordination and resources — but can help with the uptake of findings.

3. Implementing team composition

The SenseMaker process will be implemented by ...

Only an internal team — A fully outsourced external team

A SenseMaker study can be entirely outsourced. In this scenario, the organization hires a SenseMaker expert to coordinate, organize, and conduct the entire study. If the SenseMaker process is internally organized and led, the project or organization will need to invest in developing internal capacities and free up staff members' time and resources for the different phases of a SenseMaker process.

Depending on the choices made for each of these three decisions, different scenarios are possible: For example, an internally managed process-oriented study with limited participation will look quite different from an outsourced results-oriented large-scale study. Each variant comes with a set of considerations that are relevant to the preparation phase of a SenseMaker process.

Table 3. Examples of core team decision domains and responsibilities

DECISION DOMAINS	RESPONSIBILITIES
• Finalize SenseMaker process plan. • Prepare final version of signification framework. • Approve deliverables of facilitators to process payments. • Prepare final version of visualizations from primary analysis for collective interpretation events.	• Prepare the SenseMaker process plan. • Participate in all activities required to design the signification framework. • Document all the versions of the signification framework. • Support selection of, and contracts for, facilitators. • Contribute to and participate in the design and implementation of facilitators' training and final user testing. • Provide on-site support and feedback to facilitators during the first week of collection. • Follow up the collection process and provide feedback, as needed, to ensure data quality. • Review the agreed deliverables of each facilitator and approve them for processing payments. • Contribute to primary analysis and prepare all the versions of the presentation to be shared with the various stakeholders for collective interpretation events. • Contribute to the preparation of the study reports and briefs based on the agreed communication strategy.

Main Considerations

At this stage, several core decisions need to be made to create a roadmap and set boundaries on how SenseMaker will be used. Much will depend on the organizational context, the topic, whether the collection tools are to be designed from scratch, the budget, and the deadlines, as well as the capacity available for leading and coordinating the process, and for facilitating the design, collection, and sensemaking stages. Experience shows that thinking through the aspects listed below helps to ensure the SenseMaker process is built on a solid foundation.

1. Establishing the core team

A SenseMaker process requires program and MEAL expertise, as well as logistical support. The core team would ideally possess these skills. Any staff member with SenseMaker experience would be an excellent addition to the team, but if current staff have insufficient experience, it would be important to include a skilled SenseMaker practitioner in the team to advise and provide technical support.

Once the core team has been established, clarify and agree on the roles, decision domains, and responsibilities of each member. Also agree on who will lead the process, if this is not yet clear. The SenseMaker lead is responsible for overseeing and coordinating the process. Table 3 gives an example of how the domains and responsibilities of the MEAL expert team members are described.

2. Conducting a stakeholder analysis

It is important to define stakeholders and to think through the information each needs, and the way they will potentially use it.
Stakeholder analysis should also involve thinking through these questions:

- Which of the stakeholders are respondents?
- Who is collecting, and how might they benefit from the collection process?
- Which stakeholders can be engaged in collective interpretation events and how?
- How can any other stakeholders be reached through a combination of communication strategies?
- What will happen with the findings, and when will it happen?

In general, three types of stakeholders are involved: (1) facilitators of story collection and self-signification and respondents, (2) participants in the analysis and sensemaking process, and (3) people reached by broader diffusion of results and insights. Deliberate efforts are needed to think about how to engage these three groups.

3. Revising the purpose and objectives

The core team should engage with relevant leadership and technical staff to review and agree on the use of the SenseMaker process: assessment, baseline, monitoring, midterm or final evaluation, impact assessment, research, or a combination of uses.

In these discussions, decision-makers need to make it clear whether the study is exploratory in nature or has a more specific or evaluative character, as it affects the nature of the SenseMaker design. There are no clear-cut answers, but if one focus is dominant, it might affect the nature of the signification framework.

The primary purpose should then be reviewed and revised as needed, and the learning questions and specific objectives developed. Answering the following questions can help:

- Why is the study being carried out?
- What are the specific expectations?
- What overarching questions are driving the study?

SenseMaker can be used for different learning purposes. It can help to provide a general sense of what is happening within a given system or group of people. It can capture and hear the voices of a specific group of people; it can inform action and strategy. It can also generate insights to inform policy. Both the process and findings can stimulate debate and facilitate a common understanding and collective decision-making. It can provide evidence of change and trends and can support donor or project participants' accountability.

4. Deciding whether to use SenseMaker alone or with other methods

One common question is whether SenseMaker alone is sufficient to achieve what is needed, or whether it is better combined with other methods in a mixed-methods approach. SenseMaker can be combined with other data collection and evaluation methods in an efficient and powerful manner. In such cases, it is important to decide how the methods will be combined: sequentially or in parallel. SenseMaker is a hypothesis-generating method, so it is an excellent method to use as an entry point: it can then be followed by other, more structured data-collection methods.

However, there are also cases in which SenseMaker has been used successfully in parallel with quantitative survey questions or qualitative interviews and focus group discussions. If it is to be used with a survey, it is important to plan well in advance how the datasets will be merged by using a unique ID. There have also been successful examples of combining the SenseMaker method with key informant interviews, focus group discussions or participatory visualization methods. The latter enable the discussion of specific findings from SenseMaker studies with selected groups of respondents, to investigate specific topics of interest in depth and to collect additional layers of information.

CRS has also experimented with the use of semi-structured interview techniques for some follow-up MCQ signifier questions as part of the collection process, with good results. However, in such cases facilitators will need additional training, as ensuring the collection of good-quality data involves a different set of competencies. Other considerations include the extent to which the use of resources can be optimized, and how the analysis of the different datasets generated can be integrated.

5. Design and agree on the sampling strategy

The design of the SenseMaker process and tools, including the budget, is affected by the types of respondent and the estimated number of stories. More complex data collection processes have logistical and financial implications. Therefore, it is crucial at this stage to discuss whose voices the study wants to hear in order to fulfill its purpose, and to determine if there is need for comparison between crucial subgroups in the sample population.

6. Determining the sensemaking approach

Approaches to sensemaking vary considerably and depend on the purpose, expected deliverables, team capabilities, and available time and resources. Discussing this phase early on can help clarify the implementation process and timeline, including the level of training and external expertise required. A more results-oriented process will focus sensemaking on utility for programming decisions, while process-oriented application will have a sensemaking approach that develops internal capabilities. The collection process or primary analysis can be entirely outsourced to an expert or undertaken internally by an individual or a team (see implementing team composition above). Collective interpretation can be omitted, facilitated by an expert or the core team, and facilitated in collective interpretation workshops with key stakeholders or in virtual collective interpretation events. Using the findings may be limited to discussions with project teams for taking action, or multiple communication materials can be developed and tailored for different stakeholders, for different purposes (positioning, influencing, and advocacy) and communicated via different channels (see extent of stakeholder participation above).

7. Outlining a communication and use strategy

SenseMaker findings can be used to drive adaptive management, new project or program design, and accountability and changes in public, private, and civil society policies and practices. In all cases, plans to communicate and use those findings should be part of the SenseMaker process design, and should be continually considered at appropriate times throughout the process.

Many options exist to communicate findings: short or detailed written form, via an oral presentation or one-to-one communication, using video, or in an interactive platform. To kickstart initial discussions of communication, consider who needs the results, how information will be shared, and when the results are needed to still be relevant and opportune for decision-making or for influencing policy design. Once the data are collected and analyzed, the communication strategy can be further refined.

Table 4. Example of main budget items by phase and activity

	ACTIVITY
Phase: Design	• Prepare and conduct a design workshop • Create or adjust the signification framework • Translate the signification framework • Prepare training materials • Digitally configure signification framework • Procure devices for collection • Pilot test the signification framework (various interactions, depending on whether it is a new design, adjusting an existing one or simply replicated) • Digitally configure signification framework
Phase: Collection	• Decide on sampling strategy and collection approach; plan the collection process • Engage key stakeholders • Select and contract facilitators • Procure and prepare devices for collection • Prepare for facilitator training and final user testing • Run facilitator training workshop and final user testing • Test dataset export • Make SenseMaker project live and ready to facilitate the collection process • Coordinate collection logistics • Facilitate narratives and their self-signification • Coordinate and supervise facilitation process for quality assurance • Clean and prepare the dataset for analysis
Phase: Sensemaking	• Install analytical and visualization software and set up user accounts, where applicable • Train the core analysis team in use of analytical and visualization software • Conduct primary analysis • Prepare for collective interpretation workshops or sessions with stakeholders • Facilitate collective interpretation workshops with stakeholders • Conduct comprehensive analysis based on insights from collective interpretation • Prepare presentations, reports, and briefs for different stakeholders • Launch publications with findings

FEES/TIME	DIRECT COSTS
• Consultant fees (local or international) and internal staff time • Fees and per diems for facilitators during training • Partner organization staff per diems or fees, if necessary	• Design workshop: venue, catering, stationery supplies • Translation into each collection language • Transportation: flights for overseas participants or consultants; vehicle rental and fuel for pilot testing trips • Accommodation and expenses for participants • Purchase of devices to be used in the collection process • Enough photocopies of the signification framework
• Consultant fees (local or international), and internal or partner staff time • Fees or per diems for facilitators during training	• Training workshop: venue, catering, and stationery supplies • Transportation: flights for overseas participants or consultants; vehicle rental and fuel for final user testing and collection • Accommodation and expenses for facilitators and participants • Catering
• Consultant fees (local or international) and internal staff time • Per diems for stakeholders involved in collective interpretation	• Translation of narratives • (Multiple) analysis and collective interpretation events: venues, catering, and stationery supplies • Transportation costs: flights for overseas participants or consultants; local travel for participants • Accommodation and expenses for participants • Editing, translation, and layout costs for publications • Printing costs

Phase 1: Preparation

8. Agreeing the timeframe of a SenseMaker process

The time required to complete a SenseMaker process varies. If a new signification framework is being designed, it will take more time than in applications that adapt or copy an existing framework. In the former, the process may take four to eight months, with the latter taking one to two months. However, the duration will depend mainly on whether the core team is dedicated full- or part-time to the SenseMaker process and is experienced or not. Other factors that affect the time frame include:

- types of respondent and sample size;
- length and complexity of the signification framework;
- the literacy levels of respondents and the facilitation needs for collection and self-signification of the narratives;
- the accessibility to the respondents;
- the need to clean data and to undertake additional data manipulation for analysis (post-categorization, translation, and transcription of narratives);
- the scope and focus of the analysis process and whether or not collective interpretation events are included and their number;
- the core team's knowledge and experience of SenseMaker and the level of training needed for the different phases of the process.

Additional contingency time is needed as delays will be inevitable due to internal and external factors. The latter include elections, social conflict, emergency situations, and difficulty accessing respondents. Internal factors may include diversion of team members to other activities or projects, translation needs, and technical software or hardware issues.

9. Identifying additional support needed

Besides the core team, other people may play a role in the activities listed in the SenseMaker process timeline. For example, translators and transcribers may need to be hired, and assistants might be needed to enter data manually, if collection is on paper rather than using devices. There may be a need to have someone train facilitators or provide IT support, to support primary or comprehensive analysis, to facilitate collective interpretation, or to design a communications plan. To document the different roles and responsibilities of the core team and other staff or consultants who support the process, two columns can be added to Table 3: one to define the member of the core team that will ultimately be responsible for implementing the activity, and the other to list those who contribute to or support the activity.

10. Budgeting for the process

A good quality SenseMaker process undertaken at the required scale should have appropriate levels of resourcing. A realistic budget estimate is needed early to manage expectations and lay the foundation for a smooth process. Larger budget items include workshops for the design, training and sensemaking; costs for the facilitators (day rates and accommodation); and honorary costs for external consultants, if expert support is needed. Table 4 lists the main budget items by phase and activity.

11. Ensuring a SenseMaker license and other needed software

The SenseMaker software is proprietary. The Cynefin Company issues licenses for organizations and for one-off applications. These will give access to the suite of functionalities required for the digital design of the signification framework, data collection, data cleaning and analysis. If other licensed software will be used for analysis and/or reporting process, the team must have licenses to use the selected software, so it is available when the sensemaking phase starts.

12. Choosing and procuring the devices that will be used for collection

Each country and organization will have specifications that will determine what devices are suitable. The considerations include affordability, ease of use, and robustness.

13. Ensuring support from leadership

Ideally, the leadership of the project or program will be involved in key decisions about the SenseMaker process. This helps ensure ongoing support, especially if this is the first time that SenseMaker is being used. The support of leadership can motivate the core team and others involved as they pilot and learn the novelties of design, collection, and interpretation, and to ensure that team members have included the different activities in their workplans, and their time commitment is secured. The findings may not align with entrenched practices or expectations, yet this is precisely the value of SenseMaker: broadening perspectives, questioning assumptions, and sharpening insights that can trigger strategic discussions and actions. Thus, it is important to ask:

- Is there sufficient support from leadership to pilot or use a method that embraces complexity and the unexpected, and generates different kinds of results from conventional quantitative and qualitative approaches?
- Are the people involved sufficiently open to embrace new types of information and insights? Is there sufficient flexibility for the generation and use of unconventional quantitative or qualitative data?

Ethical Considerations[1]

The ethics of using SenseMaker are about keeping people safe, respecting their privacy, and maintaining high levels of integrity and transparency throughout. Each organization will have its own principles, standards and processes for ethical conduct of research or evaluation. Box 6 offers a list of ethical principles to think about what is essential. Developed for research, they can guide any inquiry. An ethical process stretches from design up to and including use of any findings.

---

1. *This section is based on Research Ethics: A Practical Guide (Oxfam 2020).*

Box 6. Example of ethical principles for research (Oxfam 2020; ESRC undated)

- Seek to maximize benefit for individuals and society and to minimize the risk and harm to any people involved.
- The rights and dignity of individuals and groups should be respected.
- Participation should be voluntary, appropriately informed and consent sought.
- All activities should be conducted with integrity and transparency.
- Lines of responsibility and accountability should be clearly defined.
- Independence should be maintained and, where conflicts of interest cannot be avoided, they should be made explicit.
- Any form of harassment, discrimination, intimidation, exploitation or abuse should be challenged.
- Do not allow the abuse of positions of power and unequal power relationships in any way.

The agreed set of ethical principles should be considered and followed throughout the SenseMaker process – when designing the process, conducting a risk analysis, selecting participants, gaining their consent, collecting data, and using the findings. All legal requirements must be followed, including data security and management. Safeguarding of all involved is paramount.

1. Designing the process. The SenseMaker process must be designed to reduce risks for participants and to increase their possible benefits from its outcome — paying particular attention to protect vulnerable participants, such as children, refugees or women.

2. Conducting a risk analysis. A risk analysis seeks to reduce unintended harm. All potential risks for all involved need identifying, with a risk mitigation strategy proposed. Updating this during the process is essential.

3. Selecting participants. Participants should only be involved if they understand the overall purpose and the process is potentially of benefit to them, directly or indirectly. Possible outcomes, such as a safer society, improved livelihoods or better working conditions in the long run, could be benefits if participants feel that is the case. Some participants may benefit simply from having had the chance to tell their story — but it is up to them to decide whether or not this is so.

4. Gaining participant consent. Facilitators must first gain informed and voluntary consent. Special care must be taken when seeking consent from vulnerable groups. The depth of this consent-taking process will depend on the topic and the extent to which it could affect participants' lives. The Collection chapter includes more details.

5. Collecting stories and other data. Facilitators should be qualified and trained for the task, including on safeguarding. They need to be self-aware and have strong listening skills. Collection should take place in places that are socially comfortable for the participant and where they are able to speak freely, and if referral is needed, they should have this information readily available.

6. Using the findings. Participants must know how their data will be used (for example, as part of the analysis and/or a public document) and must consent to this. They must be asked how much of their identity is shared, if any, and they must be free to choose this. With SenseMaker, anonymity is the norm.

7. Ensure that all legal requirements are followed. This will include following general data protection regulations, such as the European Union (EU) General Data Protection Regulation (GDPR) that applies to data collected elsewhere but used by EU-based entities. It involves ensuring that any ethical clearance with national research boards is obtained on time.

8. Data management and security. Confidentiality and consent are closely linked to data management and protection. Managing, storing and sharing personal and sensitive data securely is part of guaranteeing confidentiality, although personal data is not normally asked in SenseMaker applications. Participants need to understand how their data will be used and what their rights are with regard to accessing their data. For data collected, used or stored in the European Union, organizations must conform to the GDPR, which governs the way in which data that can identify individuals are handled, including limited timeframes for storage.

9. Safeguarding. Both Oxfam and CRS have a zero-tolerance policy towards sexual harassment, exploitation, and abuse. For any application of SenseMaker, this involves creating a safe culture for the process, monitoring the process, stopping it if needed, ensuring that any cases are reported and followed-up, committing to the safety of participants and facilitators, and training facilitators to explicitly implement safeguarding practices.

Developing the SenseMaker Process Plan

Table 5 provides a checklist for developing a SenseMaker process plan with all the activities for each phase and a timeline for each activity. Of course, it is context-specific, but it includes core activities, which can be adjusted to accommodate the customized SenseMaker process.

Table 5. Checklist for developing a timeline for the SenseMaker process

	ACTIVITY	DELIVERABLES
Phase: Design	Prepare for the design workshop	• Workshop plan • Facilitation process • Presentations, handouts, and flipcharts • Training materials, if necessary
	Design workshop	• Draft of the signification framework (V1 paper version)
	Run preliminary testing and first critical review of the signification framework	• Revised draft of the signification framework (V2 paper version)
	Run in-situ tests and second critical review	• Revised draft of signification framework (V3 paper version)
	Prepare for the digital configuration of the signification framework	• Digital version of the signification framework (V3 digital version)
Phase: Collection	Decide on collection process	• Collection plan
	Engage key stakeholders	• Agreement and commitment from all implementing partners and key stakeholders
	Select and contract facilitators	• Facilitators contracted and ready to start with training and collection
	Procure and prepare electronic devices for collection (for app-based capture)	• Application used for collection installed and signification framework downloaded.
	Prepare for the facilitator training and final user-testing	• All logistics prepared and organized • Paper version of the signification framework printed • Facilitator manual and all training materials ready and printed
	Run facilitator training workshop	• Facilitators trained
	Run user testing and final review of the signification framework	• Final version of the signification framework (V4 paper version) • Final version of the facilitator manual
	Revise the digitally configured signification framework, if needed	• Final version of the signification framework (V4 digital version)
	Run a dataset download test	• All labels and variables are showing correctly; no test observations are missing.

ACTIVITY	DELIVERABLES
Finalize logistics	• All the logistics in place to facilitate the collection process
Collect data	• Collection process facilitated and data uploaded
Coordinate and supervise the collection process and monitor data quality	• Quality data collected
Clean and prepare dataset	• Data ready for primary analysis
Ensure team members engaged in analysis have access to the dataset and the analytical or visualization software	• Core team members have all necessary software installed and user accounts set up.
Train the core team in analysis	• Core team trained in analytical approach and to use the analytical or visualization software
Conduct primary analysis	• Annotated PowerPoint presentation with findings from primary analysis
Prepare for collective interpretation workshops or sessions with selected stakeholders	• Plan for each event with background, objectives and products, list of participants, date, time and place, and agenda • Protocol for the facilitation of each event • Presentations and handouts • Flipcharts with visualizations
Facilitate collective interpretation workshops with selected stakeholders	• Insights from stakeholders' interpretation of findings, and questions for further analysis • Proposed actions in response to the findings
Conduct comprehensive analysis based on the insights from collective interpretation	• Annotated presentation with finalized findings
Preparation of presentations, reports and briefs for different stakeholders	• Findings documented in different formats for different stakeholders
Launch of the publications with findings	• Findings broadly shared with all stakeholders

Phase 2: Design

- 55 **Signification Framework Design Principles**
- 57 **The Analytical Framing of the SenseMaker Process**
- 61 **Designing the Sampling Strategy**
- 64 **Design and Structure of the Signification Framework**
- 66 **Drafting the Signification Framework**
- 86 **Testing and Critically Reviewing the Signification Framework**
- 90 **Creating and Testing the Digital Version of the Signification Framework**
- 91 **Translating the Signification Framework**

The signification framework is the basis of a SenseMaker process, as it provides the structure for the collection and signification of narratives.

Phase 2: Design

The signification framework is the basis of a SenseMaker process, as it provides the structure for the collection and signification of narratives. It consists of a set of carefully designed questions needed to prompt a narrative and to facilitate respondents' self-signification process. It is based on the analytical framing that emerges from the Preparation phase. The design of the signification framework reflects the purpose and focus of the study and guides the sensemaking process. Good signification framework design is fundamental to ensuring the quality of the SenseMaker process and the usefulness of the findings for making decisions and informing actions or policy design.

Signification Framework Design Principles

The Design phase is a critical part of a SenseMaker process because of its great impact on the relevance and quality of the findings. Whether this phase is undertaken by an individual or by the core team, it is essential to consider the different stakeholders' needs and interests. This will improve the quality of the design, its relevance, and respect for the findings, which will ensure their use in making decisions, taking action or designing policies.

The design of the signification framework needs to follow good MEAL design principles and practices. In addition, six principles particularly relevant when using SenseMaker will help ensure a high-quality design.

Principle 1. Focus on describing concrete real experience and related layers of information.

The design of the signification framework is driven by the intent to hear about day-to-day experiences of people about their lives (or what they have seen or heard about). It does not seek evaluative statements or people's opinions on particular topics or change processes—although a description of events may include reflections, evaluations, or opinions on the real events described. The prompter aims to trigger a description of the events in the manner of a narrative, and the signifier questions are developed to generate additional layers of description on top of people's narratives, providing more information about the experience.

Principle 2. Strike a balance between exploratory and focused questions.

The analytical framing, shaped by the core purpose and thematic focus of the SenseMaker inquiry, is the basis of a quality design. This includes the concepts selected to frame the SenseMaker process (such as resilience, governance, justice, and behavioral change), the elements or components related to these concepts, and the relationships among them. This analytical framing plays a key role in the design of the signifier questions. These concepts put boundaries around and give order to the inquiry. They are driven by hypotheses and assumptions. However, these focused questions need to be balanced with questions that allow the exploration of new (or unknown) concepts, elements or components of concepts, and the different relations among them. Thus, the design requires finding a proper balance of focused and exploratory signifier questions.

Principle 3. Focus on the value each question adds to come to a set of essential questions.

A signification framework will be shorter than a survey, including only those questions that add value and contribute uniquely to the analysis. The design process is not driven by asking a large number of questions that try to capture all variables of possible interest. Instead, the design team is disciplined by asking themselves whether a proposed question will add value by generating information relevant to a learning question or to the purpose of the study. A signification framework consisting of 25 questions will already provide more analytical options than there is time for. 'Less' definitely is 'more' in SenseMaker.

Principle 4. Approach the design with curiosity and be open to ambiguity.

A quality SenseMaker design will lead to the identification of emergent practices that can be scaled, or weak signals about threats that need concrete actions to stop them from escalating. These are crucial elements for fostering adaptation and innovation, and require exploring new concepts and unknowns. This means that the Design phase needs to be approached in a way that consciously seeks surprise and is open to ambiguity: a much more open-ended and nuanced approach than is often the case in more conventional methods. The SenseMaker core signifier questions, discussed in detail in this chapter, are well-suited for this, as they do not force respondents into the either-or framing of MCQs. This is especially important, as people do not live in terms of either-or options. People's decisions, actions, and feelings are driven by multiple simultaneous options, and these types of signifier questions recognize the ambiguity and nuance embedded in people's lives.

Principle 5. Seek clarity on how SenseMaker complements other monitoring, evaluation, and research methods.

SenseMaker can be used as a stand-alone method, but it is often used in combination with other MEAL or research methods. The team needs to be clear whether SenseMaker is expected to fill information gaps or to triangulate with other findings. Before designing the signification framework, spend time reviewing existing MEAL or research processes to determine what information gaps are suited to being filled using SenseMaker, or where uncertain findings need triangulating.

Principle 6. Ensure rigorous testing and critical review prior to use.

The prompter and the follow-up core SenseMaker signifier questions require rigorous testing and critical review. This is an essential part of the design, given the nature of these questions. Checking that all topics of interest and concepts in the analytical framing are covered by the final question set is a good first step. When designing the prompter and follow-up signifier questions, it is important to ensure that design recommendations—as explained in detail later in this chapter—are used to check the quality of the questions. Making sure that several prompters are tested will ensure that the final version of the prompter produces the kind of narratives that will be useful for the SenseMaker process. Testing the signifier questions will ensure clear wording to obtain accurate responses. This is especially important when translations are needed, to ensure that the meaning of the questions is not lost. It is also important to test the sequence of questions, in order to evoke a coherent and smoothly flowing conversation based on the framework. Sometimes questions do not result in the kind of data needed for the Sensemaking phase. Testing the signification framework by entering and analyzing fictional data—and using this to conduct some primary or comprehensive analysis—can help show the type of findings that are possible and to what extent these findings will address the learning questions.

The Analytical Framing of the SenseMaker Process

The analytical framing is the bedrock of a quality SenseMaker process, guiding the entire design and sensemaking process. Deciding on the analytical framing is good practice for any MEAL process and essential for any research process. It is particularly important in SenseMaker, as it defines the concepts that will be explored and the linkages between these concepts that inform the design of the signification framework. As this is less about asking direct questions, the selection, adjustment, and development of concepts and relationships between them are critical steps.

There are at least three types of input that can be used to frame the SenseMaker design and sensemaking. Each type of input can be used on its own or have more influence than others, but usually a combination of the three inputs are used to create the analytical framing of the SenseMaker process. The three types are:

- **Thematic field theory:** Existing theories and concepts of the area of study described in the literature, including their respective conceptual and analytical frameworks.
- **Theory of change:** Intervention rationale or other program design models of the specific initiative or project.
- **Experiential knowledge:** Different perceptions, experiences, interests and knowledge of involved stakeholders, related to the topic of interest, including those of the respondents themselves.

Thematic field theory

Building on the theoretical and conceptual knowledge related to a field of expertise or topic of interest provides clear guidance for the conceptual framing of the signifier questions. The first step, then, is to review the literature and consult content experts on the thematic focus and scope of the SenseMaker process. Topics such as resilience, nutrition, gender, girls' empowerment, food systems, value chains, inclusive business, capacity development, peacebuilding, conflict prevention, and social psychology—among other fields of study—are well-researched and have existing conceptual and analytical frameworks.

Based on a review of the existing literature in the topic of interest, the SenseMaker core team, in consultation with thematic experts, can select or adapt an existing analytical framework; or they may also decide to develop one if none of the existing ones fit the purpose. Be aware, however, that the latter requires more time and effort. Another factor to consider is interaction with different stakeholders who have practical experience in and knowledge of the thematic focus. This is very important for ensuring that the analytical framework selected, adapted, or developed is grounded in practice and easily understood.

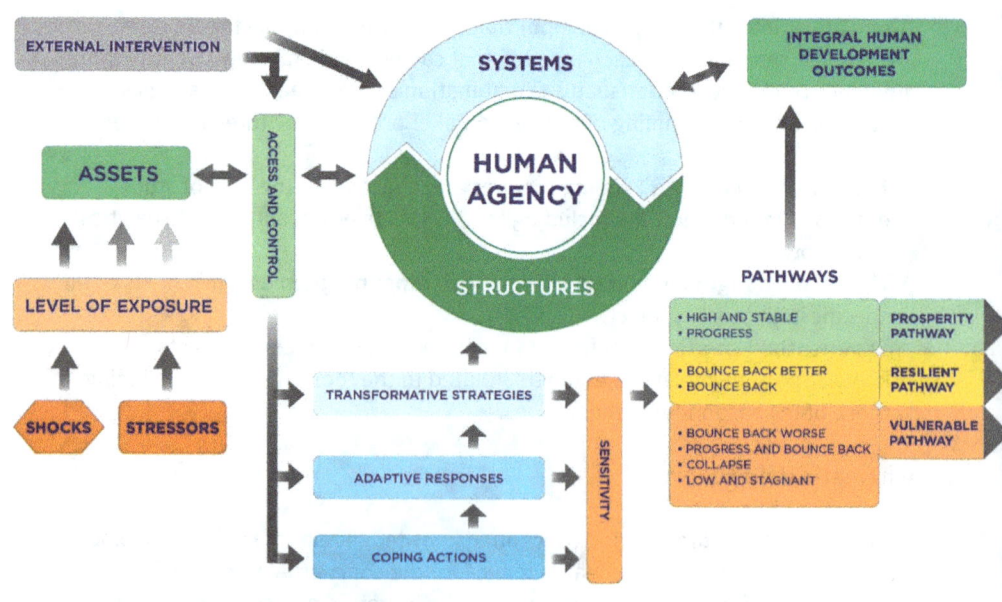

Figure 8. CRS analytical framework developed to assess 'pathways to prosperity' and resilience capabilities

There are several examples of how adjusting or adapting analytical frameworks based on a review of the literature or frameworks has yielded stronger results for development interventions. For example, a literature review helped reveal how concepts such as 'agency', 'voice', and 'value' relate to how girls in Ethiopia and Rwanda experience their girlhood and their sense of power in shaping their own lives. Winnowing out these concepts helped the organization Girl Hub (now Girl Effect) to reflect on its strategy and to identify a limited number of thematic priorities to help improve girls' lives.

Another organization, Rikolto International, designed what is called the Inclusive Business Scan, which assesses and generates insights about the inclusivity of business models and practices used by buyers in smallholder value chains. The scan was based on five inclusive business principles included in the LINK methodology, developed by the International Center for Tropical Agriculture (CIAT). The Inclusive Business Scan helps to adjust interventions for value chains, provides feedback to buyers and farmer organizations, and stimulates dialogue among value-chain actors. CRS wanted to assess advances along what the organization calls the 'pathway to prosperity', and the resilience capabilities of farming households to recuperate from shocks and stressors. To inform the SenseMaker study, CRS developed a resilience analytical framework based on the resilience frameworks of the Institute of Development Studies, TANGO International, the Department for International Development, and the United States Agency for International Development (Frankenberger et al. 2012; USAID 2013; Brooks et al. 2014; Béné et al. 2015). These were adapted using the analytical framework proposed by Gottret (2007) and the experiences of CRS staff in implementing resilience-strengthening projects. The final analytical framework (Figure 8) was fundamental to the design of the signification framework used to conduct ten case studies across nine countries. These studies, conducted between 2015 and 2018, helped to assess advances along the 'pathway to prosperity', the vulnerabilities faced by rural families and their resilience capabilities, as well as the factors that contributed to, or hindered, their ability to follow prosperous and resilient pathways.

Theory of change

In programmatic contexts, theories of change or logical models—such as the logic framework or results framework—that include goals, strategic objectives, intermediate results or outcomes, outputs, critical assumptions, and corresponding indicators are commonly used to guide interventions and frame MEAL processes. Making the programming design rationale behind these models explicit is very useful in the design and sensemaking phases.

When SenseMaker is used for MEAL purposes, the theory of change and logical models are often the dominant theory used to frame the SenseMaker process. If the program theories include evaluation or learning questions, these components can also provide important direction for the focus and scope of the SenseMaker process. For example, the CRS project on conflict prevention in the Philippines was partly framed around elements of the results framework (the logical model) and a set of learning questions. The signification framework of a youth empowerment project implemented by Via Don Bosco in Bolivia and Madagascar was also linked to the indicators of the logic framework. The theory of change and the set of evaluation questions framed the design of the signification framework and the sensemaking process in an evaluation of a value chain program funded by IFAD in Cameroon.

Experiential knowledge

The perceptions, experiences, and interests of the stakeholders involved are very useful to inform the process. Experienced staff, participants or content experts are invited to contribute to the design process and bring in their personal experiences. Their expertise on context and content can help ensure the design responds to the needs of the SenseMaker process stakeholders.

The Inclusive Business Scan developed by Rikolto International was based on the LINK methodology analytical framework (Lundy et al. 2014). Involving technical and methodological experts, people familiar with the local context, and the respondents themselves in the design of the SenseMaker process was fundamental to a robust design. This allowed forgotten dimensions to be easily spotted and brought nuance to specific questions, focusing on the information needs of the different stakeholders.

In the CRS-led SenseMaker 'pathway to prosperity' example, the involvement of technical experts and staff helped adjust the analytical frameworks found in the literature: They placed human agency at the center, recognizing that project participants are not passive recipients of aid but active agents whose decisions, strategies, and actions shape their own development. The concept of human agency thus was included to assess project participants' capacity to cope and to pursue their goals. In addition, concepts of systems and structures that affect what people can do and how they do it were also introduced. This gave a tailored design that responded to different information needs.

Designing the Sampling Strategy

A crucial aspect during the preparation of a SenseMaker process relates to the design of the sampling strategy. This involves determining whose voices the study needs to hear to fulfill its purpose, which in turn will define the study population. Once this population has been specified, the next step is to determine how it needs to be grouped or stratified to ensure that useful comparisons between groups of respondents can be made during the Sensemaking phase. A general principle is that a sample should be large enough to provide the answer to the research question, while also being sufficiently small to keep the process in budget. Non-probability sampling strategies, where the respondents are not randomly selected and the probability that the sample is representative of the population is unknown, are convenient and inexpensive, but do not allow for generalization to the studied population.

If the aim of the study is to generalize the conclusions to the study population, a statistically robust sampling method should be used. This requires a standard sampling procedure based on the desired confidence level (the probability that the value of a variable falls within a specified range of values) and the accepted error margin (the radius, or half the width, of a confidence interval for a particular variable).

As with any method, a second consideration relates to whether the study aims to compare different groups of the population with the intent of drawing conclusions about the similarities or differences between them. Studies usually aim to compare respondents by sex or age group, by geographical area (e.g. a region facing severe climatic stressors with a region facing minor climatic stressors), or by whether they have received services from a development project, thus requiring a stratified sampling strategy. This sampling strategy has the advantage that these subgroups of the population tend to be more homogenous, and so a smaller sample is needed to properly generalize the conclusions. This also enables an assessment of whether the similarities or differences that are found between the subgroups of interest are statistically significant.

In addition to the above basic sampling principles valid for any method, another important consideration for selecting a sampling strategy for a SenseMaker process is the importance of having a sufficiently large number of respondents in each subgroup of interest. This is important, as sensemaking relies greatly on visualizing patterns of responses, which might not be possible if there are very few responses for a specific subgroup. In addition, comparing visualizations between two groups with different numbers of responses can be tricky. For example, a histogram resulting from responses to a slider signifier question for a subgroup with more responses will have higher bars than a histogram from a subgroup with fewer responses. Similarly, the dominant pattern in a triad signifier question for a subgroup with more responses will have a higher density of dots than the dominant pattern for another subgroup with fewer responses.

Another consideration specific to SenseMaker when designing the sampling strategy is that, if the purpose of the SenseMaker process is only to observe a general pattern, describe a particular group in an exploratory way, and gain an overall understanding of the context and the main perspectives, it is unlikely that there will be a need for a representative sample. When SenseMaker is used for monitoring

Table 6. Sampling strategies and their implications for sensemaking

	RESPONDENTS	EXAMPLES	SUITABLE ANALYSIS APPROACH AND SIGNIFICATION FRAMEWORK DESIGN CONSIDERATIONS
Sampling strategy: Census	Entire population	Refugees that graduated from a vocational training program; girls that participated in village-based play centers (e.g. 30 centers with 20–25 girls each); members of a cooperative (e.g. 300 cacao farmers); or all project participants for continuous monitoring purposes	**Visualization and basic pattern detections:** Possible **Statistical analysis:** As the whole population is interviewed, findings can be generalized by default to the study population and statistical tests are valid. **Text analysis:** Possible
Sampling strategy: Intentional sample	Responses are collected from an equal number of respondents from each group or segment of interest (e.g. female versus male farmers, fathers versus mothers, younger versus older girls).	For the final evaluation of a refugee program in Ecuador, a sample of the population of project participants was estimated at N = 480, giving a 95% confidence level and 5% margin of error. In addition, there was a need to ensure a sufficient number of stories to allow for a meaningful visual pattern analysis across three subgroups within the refugee population. A sample was randomly selected from a list of each group of participants to ensure a minimum of 80 people, representative of each group.	**Visualization and basic pattern detections:** Possible **Statistical analysis:** As the sample is representative of the studied population, findings from the sample can be generalized to that population. In addition, comparison between groups is possible, but only when it is possible to adjust or weight the sample after collection to make it representative of the population. **Text analysis:** Possible

purposes, with the aim of collecting data during implementation, there may be no need to have a defined sample size.

More information on sampling strategies and their implications for sensemaking is provided in Table 6.

	RESPONDENTS	EXAMPLES	SUITABLE ANALYSIS APPROACH AND SIGNIFICATION FRAMEWORK DESIGN CONSIDERATIONS
Sampling strategy: Representative sample	Sample is representative of the overall population, as statistical approaches are used to define the sample size. If SenseMaker is used in parallel with survey questionnaires, the sample size for SenseMaker is often aligned with that of the survey.	A population census was conducted in three targeted health zones as part of a project in the DRC. The census lists were then used to draw a stratified sample (per health zone) with N = 606, giving a 98% confidence level and 5% margin of error.	**Visualization and basic pattern detections:** Possible **Statistical analysis:** As the sample is representative of the studied population, findings can be generalized to that population. In addition, the stratified sample allows statistical tests to be conducted in order to assess differences and similarities between the subgroups of the populations. **Text analysis:** Possible
Sampling strategy: Undefined sample	Responses are collected from an undefined sample. Suitable for monitoring; where there are no opportunities to collect from a representative sample or certain groups; where a qualitative approach to data analysis is taken; or where there are very few respondents in a population.	Continuous collection of data on the perception of capacity strengthening from internal staff and external partners. Data collected during workshops globally.	**Visualization and basic pattern detections:** Possible **Statistical analysis:** Possible, but only when the sample can be adjusted or weighted after collection to make it representative of the population. **Text analysis:** Possible

Design and Structure of the Signification Framework

The process for designing a new signification framework begins by drafting possible questions, either through a design workshop with multiple stakeholders or by working with the design team. Once the design team has a common understanding of the use and purpose of the SenseMaker process, learning questions, sampling strategy, and analytical framing, a first version of the signification framework can be drafted. Where available and suitable, a signification framework that has been used for a similar SenseMaker process, serving similar objectives, can be adapted to fit the purpose of the new process. This can avoid the drafting of the initial questions and preliminary testing. If a SenseMaker process is repeated in a different setting, an existing framework can be replicated. This will require only minor customization, user testing, and revision. The process of designing the signification framework for the different scenarios (creation, adaptation, or replication) is presented in Figure 9.

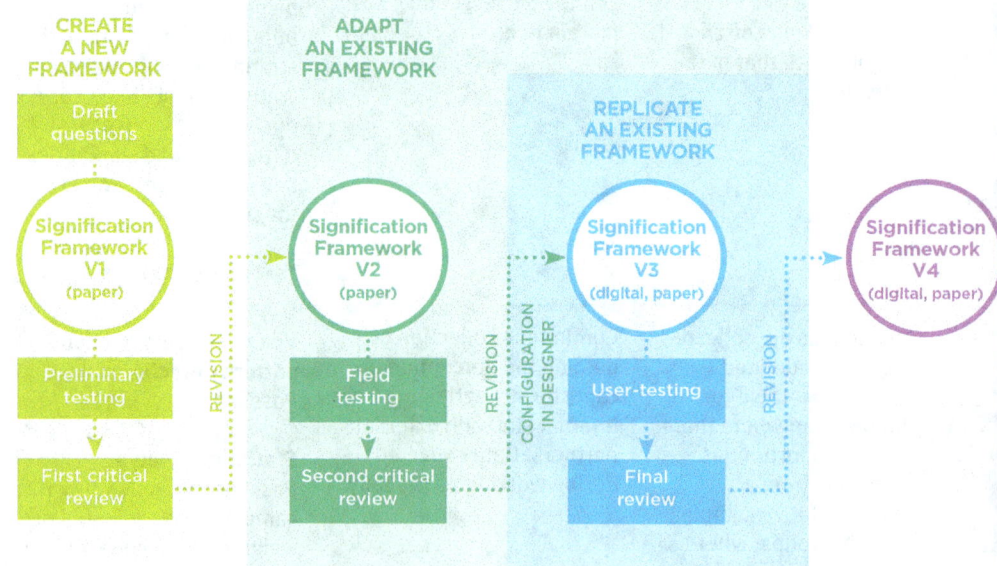

Figure 9. Process of designing the signification framework (new or adapting an existing one)

A standard signification framework includes the prompter, the story title question, the signifier questions, the sociodemographic aspects of respondents and their context, and collection protocol questions. While some question types used in the signification framework (like MCQs) are common, others are specific to SenseMaker, forming the core of the self-signification process. These are the triad, slider, slider-with-stones, and canvas-with-stones questions. These question types are described in detail in this chapter, together with design recommendations and practical examples. Table 7 presents the question types and their specific purposes in the signification framework.

Table 7. Overview of question types for signification frameworks

Purpose	Open-ended questions	Core SenseMaker questions (triad, slider/stone)	MCQs
NARRATIVE QUESTIONS Generate a story and a title. These include (1) a 'prompter' question to trigger the memory of a specific experience or event of personal significance, related to the topic of interest that generates the narrative; and (2) a 'title' question to generate significant key words that the respondent associates with the experience, to give a title to the narrative.	✓		
SIGNIFIER QUESTIONS Adds meaning to the experience shared in the narrative, providing additional layers of information about it.	✓	✓	✓
DEMOGRAPHIC AND CONTEXT QUESTIONS Provides information about the respondents and their context. Enables disaggregation of the analysis among different groups of respondents for comparison purposes.	✓		✓
COLLECTION PROTOCOL QUESTIONS Helps track key aspects of collection (time and location, respondent ID or survey ID, facilitator ID), and ensures all necessary consent protocols for ethical collection.	✓		✓

Drafting the Signification Framework

There are a few important considerations to keep in mind before and during the drafting of the signification framework.

Length of the signification framework. SenseMaker-specific signifier questions lie at the core of the method. They are designed to encourage the respondent to reflect on their responses, and to ensure that respondents remain focused on the self-signification process prompted by these questions. So that data quality is not compromised, it is good practice to keep the signification framework as short as possible, without compromising its potential value.

Sequencing the questions. After a short introduction and collection protocol questions, there is an open-ended prompter to trigger a narrative, followed by a question that prompts the respondent to give the narrative a title. After the respondent has shared the narrative, they are asked to self-interpret their stories by answering a set of signifier questions. The order of these questions can vary. Some choose to organize the questions by type, while others organize them thematically to follow an ordered conversation. It is common to end with the sets of sociodemographic and context questions. If the SenseMaker interview is combined with a survey, the recommendation is to start with the former, as the survey questions could affect the story shared.

Phrasing signifier questions. All signifier questions relate and give significance to the experience; they should thus start with a reference to the experience that the respondents have previously shared. For example, questions can begin with 'In the story you have just shared...' or 'In the experience shared...' or similar. This reminds respondents that their answers relate to the experiences they described in their narratives, and they are not being asked a general opinion.

Opt-out options. Some signification framework questions should include a 'not applicable' option. In some countries, or when an institutional review board for ethics in research is required, it is necessary to include a 'prefer not to answer' option.

Establishing and training the design team. In the Design phase, the core team will work with other stakeholders, forming a design team, which may not have full knowledge of the SenseMaker process. It is important, therefore, to ensure that all members of the design team:
- are trained in the basics of SenseMaker, and have a shared understanding of how SenseMaker works, compared to other quantitative and qualitative methods;
- fully understand the different types of SenseMaker-specific core questions—triads, sliders, sliders with stones, canvases with stones, and MCQs—and when to use each of them. This chapter includes detailed explanations of each type of question, as well as guidance and recommendations to make proper use of them, with examples from different SenseMaker processes.

Drafting the signification framework involves four steps, which are now described in detail.

Step 1. Generating concepts

The signification framework is designed around the concepts that the study wants to understand and elements of these concepts. The identification of the concepts is often referred to as 'unpacking' the topic at hand. These concepts are derived from the analytical framing of the study, which is informed by the three types of inputs discussed in Phase 1: Preparation: thematic field theory, theory of change and experiential knowledge.

Examples of concepts include drivers, temporal orientation, identity, power, pattern of behavior or action, dependency or loyalty, and associated feelings. 'Unpacking' refers to identifying the dimensions that are at play in each of the concepts; these can be highly contextual or generic with different options depending on how the concept is approached. For example, drivers of experiences of conflict can be very diverse and context-specific, including, for example, religious, ethnic, political, resource-based, and combinations of these. Another way of looking at conflict drivers could be to ask whether conflict is caused by personal beliefs, laws or rules, or cultural patterns; one could also investigate the main actors that have caused the conflict and continue to exert an influence over it. These different ways of looking at drivers of conflict will lead to different questions and different types of questions (sliders, triads, multiple-choice questions, stones questions, see next section).

An overview of the concepts (derived from the analytical framing) and the corresponding dimensions is a practical approach that enhances the quality of the signification framework. Box 7 provides some examples of how the analytical framing inspired different signification frameworks.

Box 7. Examples from practice to frame the design

- The different concepts in the resilience analytical framework developed by CRS (Figure 8), its respective elements, and the relation among them, were reflected in a set of signifier questions designed to assess resilience capabilities and progress along an assumed 'pathway to prosperity', and how different coping actions, adaptive responses and transformative strategies contributed to these outcomes in eight countries of Latin America, East Africa, and South East Asia.

- Via Don Bosco used a conceptual model on the empowerment of vulnerable youth in Bolivia and Madagascar, which included three dimensions of empowerment (personal, relational, and behavioral) linked to the indicators of the logical framework as the basis for framing the design of a signification framework to understand and measure the empowerment of vulnerable youth and, at a later stage, to structure the sensemaking process.

- The Tipping Point program, implemented by CARE USA, used its theory of change and social norms framework as the foundation for the design of signifier questions to understand the challenges that adolescent girls face in Bangladesh.

- CRS' A3B peacebuilding project in Mindanao in the Philippines used a combination of learning questions, the project's theory of change and results framework, and inputs from project partners and peacebuilding experts to draft a signification framework aimed at understanding how people perceive the influence of peace and conflict situations on relationships, level of trust, and feelings of safety in their communities.

- Oxfam used the Ethical Trading Initiative core principles and its program strategy assumptions as the foundational concepts in designing a signification framework to conduct a labor rights study with the aim of assessing interim progress on principles such as dignity, safety, and security in an African country.

- The Holiday Participation Centre in Flanders, Belgium took an exploratory approach and used the perspectives of network members and stakeholders to select the key concepts that framed the design of a signification framework to understand the drivers, dynamics, and challenges relating to how holidays could be made possible for people in poverty in Flanders.

- Oxfam's People on the Move studies in the Central African Republic and Iraq made use of commonly held public assumptions about refugees, concepts used in displacement-related global debates, concepts relating to livelihoods and resilience, and Oxfam's gender justice focus to prioritize the key concepts that were used in a signification framework developed to understand the needs of displaced people.

- CRS employed competency models—which included the competencies to be developed and strengthened by their agriculture and livelihood program and the behavioral evidences that need to be demonstrated to achieve these competencies—as the basis for the design of signification frameworks that would assess behavioral changes promoted by training, coaching, and mentoring activities using its SMART skills approach, in five projects in Malawi, Zambia, Ethiopia, Guatemala, El Salvador, Honduras and Nicaragua.

Step 2: Drafting narrative questions (prompt and title)

One feature that differentiates SenseMaker from most other methods is its use of a personal narrative shared by respondents. That experience of personal significance, and the few key words that describe it, are elicited as responses to two open-ended questions: the prompter and the title question.

The prompter has the following characteristics:

- It should trigger the respondent's memory of a specific, concrete and lived experience or event, or elicit descriptions of a change process in their life or community, that is related to the thematic focus of the SenseMaker process. The question should not elicit an evaluative statement or opinion about an issue: what is wanted is a description of the succession of events, decisions and actions taken, and their outcomes, providing a complete narrative of the experience and the people involved in it.
- It should be neutral, inviting both negative and positive experiences (unless multiple prompter are used, allowing choice among them).
- It should specify a timeline within which the experience would have taken place, if applicable (e.g. 'recent', 'in the last year', 'during the participation in a specific program or project'). The more recent the event, the more likely the respondent is to remember it, making the response more reliable. If a more specific timeline is needed for analysis, a follow-up MCQ signifier can be used (e.g. 'When did this experience occur?' – 'Less than 6 months ago', 'More than 6 months ago').

The design of the prompters determines the thematic focus, length, and level of detail of narratives. Where the text of narratives will be important for analytical purposes, the question must be broad enough to prompt an informative and complete narrative, while also being specific enough to generate a narrative related to the thematic focus. When the narrative will be used only as an entry point to trigger a memory of a specific event, there is no need to focus on capturing an informative and complete narrative. As a principle, prompter should be clear enough to generate the desired type of narratives without any further clarification. Examples of prompters designed for different purposes are shown in Table 8.

The prompter is followed by a title question that helps respondents describe the experience they shared in a few key words. For example, the following question can be used to prompt a title for the narrative: 'When thinking about the story you have just shared, which three to five words came to mind?'

In some studies, multiple prompts are used, and respondents can choose the prompt they wish to respond to. Different prompts can also be used for different respondent groups, while the rest of the questions remain the same. This allows a comparison between multiple perspectives on the same issues (e.g. students versus teachers). For example, the CRS Population, Migration, and Refugees project in Ecuador worked with refugees from Colombia and Venezuela, as well as with vulnerable populations in Ecuador. The prompt used to conduct a final evaluation of the project was slightly different for refugees than for the vulnerable Ecuadorians.

Table 8. Examples and purposes of prompters

PROMPT: *Think about an important experience (positive or negative) that you had in your work in agriculture or livestock, which significantly influenced your household's well-being, and that you would like to share with your grandchildren. What story would you tell them?* **Purpose:** Assess the impact of 17 years of implementing an agriculture and livelihoods program on promoting farm families' advancement along a 'pathway to prosperity'.

PROMPT: *Please share a recent experience (within the past six months) about a challenge that you or another girl in your village faced and how you or she dealt with this challenge. What happened? Who was involved? How did the situation end?* **Purpose:** Understand the effects of a girls' empowerment program and inform the design of the second phase of a program in Bangladesh.

PROMPT: *Since you have become a member of the cooperative, can you tell us about an important positive or negative change related to the production, processing or selling/marketing of your crop (onions, rice, or cassava) and how this has affected you and your family? Describe what happened.* **Purpose:** Evaluate a value-chain project in Cameroon.

PROMPT: *Provide a short summary of your recent experience as a recipient of a capacity strengthening activity (your experience may be positive, neutral or negative).* **Purpose:** Monitor and elicit continual feedback from partner capacity strengthening activities globally.

PROMPT: *Describe a recent experience or situation that made you feel motivated or discouraged about your professional future. Describe what happened (What? When? Who?)* **Purpose:** Conduct a baseline and midterm evaluation of a technical and vocational education and training program in Madagascar and Bolivia for a program aimed at empowering vulnerable youth.

PROMPT: *Think of a specific moment that happened in the last six months when you felt particularly encouraged or concerned about producing coffee and selling it to [a company]. Describe what happened?* **Purpose:** Assess the inclusivity of business models and practices applied by buyers in smallholder value chains in order to adjust value-chain support interventions, provide feedback to buyers and farmer organizations, and stimulate dialogue among value chain actors.

PROMPT: *Share the experience that drastically influenced your well-being, or that of your family, and prompted you to make the decision to [cross the Ecuadorian border and] ask for support from the Scalabrini Mission. What triggered this situation? What did you do to overcome it? How did the Scalabrini Mission support you and with what results?* **Purpose:** Evaluate the Population, Refugees, and Migration project in terms of the well-being of refugees and their social and economic integration into host communities.

A 'title' question (see Table 9) seeks to encourage respondents to summarize or describe their story in a few words. Titles summarize a story, give an indication of what stories are about, and highlight any message most valuable to the respondent. All of these can help understand the themes and issues the respondents are raising.

Table 9. Examples of title questions

If you were to give this situation a title or describe it in a few words, how would you title or describe it?	*What #hashtag label would you use to describe your story?*
Please give your story a title.	*What caption(s) would you use to describe your story?*
If you were to describe your story in a few key words or give it a headline, what would they be?	*Please describe your story in a few key words.*

Step 3: Drafting core SenseMaker signifier questions

After the respondents have shared their experience, they are asked to answer a set of follow-up questions, many of which are signifier questions. Signifier questions can include core SenseMaker questions (triads, sliders, sliders with stones, and canvases with stones), as well as open-ended questions and MCQs. These questions prompt the respondents to provide additional layers of meaning to the experiences shared in their narratives; this is referred to as the self-signification process. The process allows the 'coding' of qualitative information about narratives, but the coding here is undertaken by the respondents, not by external evaluators, researchers, or experts, reducing their intermediation.

To design signifier questions that generate useful, relevant insights, design team members should possess a solid understanding of the different types of questions, their objectives, and design principles. The following tables provide detailed design recommendations and examples from practice of each type of core SenseMaker-specific signifier question.

Designing slider signifier questions

A slider is a horizontal line with one element of a concept at each end, and one issue that can be placed on the line. It indicates the relative strength of two elements of the same concept or different concepts. Respondents answer by positioning their response somewhere between the two extremes. There are different slider question variations for different purposes (see Table 10 for variations and Table 11 for related examples).

Table 10. Variations, design recommendations, and data format generated for slider questions

Design recommendations

Sliders are not meant to replace or serve as MCQs or Likert scale questions, where responses are scored along a range (such as 1–10), and which are easy to game. Only one element should be provided at each end of the slider, otherwise a respondent could become confused as to what is being evaluated. For example, if one extreme is 'natural resources were in very good condition and well managed' and the other extreme is 'natural resources were in bad condition and poorly managed', it will not be clear what the respondent should answer if, for example, natural resources were in good condition but poorly managed.

Sliders are easy questions to respond to, can be very useful for insight generation, and do not take a lot of facilitation time. However, if too many sliders are developed, the team must critically assess which are necessary and then prioritize them accordingly. It is recommended to have no more than four slider questions in one signification framework.

Data format generated

Pattern visualization of each continuum.
Quantitative data are captured by an X-coordinate value that ranges from 0 to 100, from left to right. Two additional values are provided indicating how close the response is to each of the extremes. The larger the number, the closer the response is to that extreme.

Table 11. Examples of slider signifier questions

Variations

Opposing extremes: In this variation, the ends of the continuum are labeled with opposite values that are presented as either both negative, both neutral, or both positive. For example, 'girls were treated too harshly' (negative) and 'girls were treated too gently' (negative). In this slider variation, a midpoint may represent an ideal situation. The question design helps to minimize gaming, as there is no obvious right or preferred answer.

In this story...

Girls are treated too harshly — Girls are spoiled and treated too softly

continued →

Table 11 continued. Examples of slider signifier questions

Continuous scale: The ends of the continuum are labeled with opposite values. The respondents are required to place a mark on the point of the scale that best reflects the experience they shared. This slider variation is used to assess the current state, direction, or extent of change from 'very negative' to 'very positive' over time. The ideal situation here is represented by one extreme and is easier to game.

The experience you shared generated changes (positive or negative) in your income…

|⎯⎯⎯⎯⎯⎯⎯⎯⎯⎯⎯○⎯⎯⎯⎯⎯⎯⎯⎯⎯⎯⎯|

Very negative change .... Very positive change

Blending elements: As a variation of the continuous scale, this slider can help generate more reflection on and nuances about a concept. For example, the outcome of loans on a continuous scale, from 'vicious cycle of indebtedness and asset loss' to 'virtuous cycle of recovery and asset building'. Even though the preferred extreme is obvious, the question requires respondents to carefully reflect on both options to choose what position along the continuum best reflects their experience.

In the experience you shared, taking a loan…

|⎯⎯⎯⎯⎯⎯⎯⎯⎯⎯⎯○⎯⎯⎯⎯⎯⎯⎯⎯⎯⎯⎯|

Led you to a great loss that negatively affected your farming or entrepreneurial activities .... Allowed you to greatly improve your farming or grow your entrepreneurial activities

Different elements of a concept: In this variation, slider labels present two different elements of a concept; or in some cases two elements of different concepts. For example, understanding a cost–benefit outcome of a decision to introduce a specific crop. The data generated by this slider variation can help to understand the outcome of decisions and to monitor how these change over time or following an intervention.

In the experience you shared, adding new crops to your land was…

|⎯⎯⎯⎯⎯⎯⎯⎯⎯⎯⎯○⎯⎯⎯⎯⎯⎯⎯⎯⎯⎯⎯|

Extremely costly .... Highly beneficial

Designing slider-with-stones signifier questions

The slider with stones is a horizontal line with one element at each extreme and multiple issues (referred to as 'stones') that can be placed along the line. It aims to determine which options are present in the experiences shared by the respondents and to assess the relative strength of the same two elements for each of the selected options.

Table 12. Variations, design recommendations, and data format generated for slider-with-stones questions

Variations

In addition to the slider variations explained in the previous section, sliders with stones can be classified by the type of stones used.

Chronological stones: Stones represent time periods that the respondent is asked to place on a continuum. For example, a slider with stones was used to reconstruct the pathways taken by farm families as a result of the change processes promoted by development interventions. Respondents were asked to place three stones – representing before, during and after the experience- on a continuous scale from 'very vulnerable' to 'very prosperous' to describe their lives during these three periods.

Practice/outcome-related stones: This variation helps to assess the presence or absence of different practices (options) and to evaluate the outcomes of these practices by placing them on a continuum. For example, a slider with stones was developed (1) to determine whether any transformational changes that result in resilience capabilities were present, and (2) to understand whether these changes, if present, led to positive or negative outcomes, as perceived by the respondents. A manageable number of five stones included: individual behaviors, collective beliefs and practices, organizational practices, private business practices, and government policies.

Actor-related stones: This variation uses stones that represent actors to assess the presence or absence of different actors and their impact. For example, in a study aimed to assess changes in farmers' organization skills and the outcomes of these changes, a slider with stones was used to assess the extent to which different types of actors (women, men, and youths) committed to achieving the agreed-on organizational goals.

Behavior/norms-related stones: This variation helps to understand behaviors or norms that influenced respondents' actions in the experiences shared. For example, in a study to evaluate efforts to influence behavior changes, a slider with stones was used to assess: (1) if respondents acted based on a few negative and related positive norms, and (2) the extent to which they acted based on these norms because of their personal norms or social norms.

Respondents answer by selecting the issues that are relevant to the experiences they have shared from a predefined list of options. They then indicate where each of these options sits between the two extreme ends of the slider.

Sliders with stones add complexity to the signification framework, both for data collection and during analysis. It is a useful type of question, though not a necessary element in every framework. Several options are possible (see Tables 12 and 13 for examples).

Design recommendations

The recommendations for slider questions apply to slider-with-stones questions with several additions.

It is not advisable to have issues that are too generic or too granular for people to place on a line. For example, people may have difficulty responding to an option such as 'improved practices' in a continuum of extremes between 'very positive results' and 'very negative results' if they have adopted different improved practices with different results. In addition, the findings will be too ambiguous for a project team to use in determining which improved practices to bring to scale. On the other hand, listing every single 'improved practice' as an option may provide too much detail, for which a multiple-choice question might be better.

Limit the number of stones to a minimum (perhaps three to six). Every issue in a slider with stones requires a respondent to take additional time to respond.

From a technical perspective, for app collection, devices that run iOS have proven more reliable and easier to use than Android devices, which can fail to properly display background images or more than five response options to these question types.

Data format generated

Pattern visualization for each option or stone.

Quantitative data for each option or stone is captured as an X-coordinate value that ranges from 0 to 100 from left to right. Two additional values are provided, indicating how close the response is to each one of the extremes. The larger the number, the closer the response is to that extreme.

Table 13. Examples of slider-with-stones signifier questions

Time-based stones	**Thinking back on the experience you shared, how did you feel?** 1. Before the experience 2. During the experience 3. After the experience Very vulnerable ←――――――――――――→ Very prosperous
Issue-based stones	**In the experience that you shared, changes in…** 1. Individual behaviors 2. Collective beliefs and practices 3. Organizational practices 4. Private business practices 5. Government policies Led to very positive results ←――――――――――――→ Led to very negative results
Actor-based stones	*In the experience shared, how did the following members of the group contribute to achieving the group's agreed goals?* 1. Female members 2. Male members 3. Younger members Not at all ←――――――――――――→ Fully
Behavior/ norm-based stones	*In the experience shared, did you act based on the following beliefs, and if so, why?* 1. Only men can take good decisions for their household 2. Men belong to the public sphere and women to the private sphere 3. Men who share tasks with their wives are considered weak You believe it to be correct ←――――――――――――→ Community members believed it to be correct

Designing canvas-with-stones signifier questions

A canvas with stones is a rectangle representing one concept on a continuous scale along two axes and various issues (stones) that can be placed on the canvas. It aims to determine which issues are relevant for the respondent, comparing various issues in terms of how they relate to each of the dimensions of a concept represented on the axes.

The respondent is asked to select issues (stones) that are relevant to the experience they shared. These stones are selected from a predefined list of options and the respondent indicates where each selected option or stone sits on the canvas. Canvases with stones take longer to answer and may be difficult for some respondents to grasp. This is because they ask the respondent to think about two dimensions at the same time and to provide a nuanced answer about the story context. This question type is not necessarily a part of every signification framework. Several options are possible (see Tables 14 and 15).

Table 14. Variations, design recommendations and data format generated for canvas-with-stones questions

Variations

Issue-based stones: For example, to assess how changes in the health of an ecosystem relates to how users manage specific natural resources, with each resource being one stone. The state of natural resources is affected by people's resource management; looking at how the two issues are related merits the use of this question type.

Actor-based stones: For example, to understand how the commitment and power of key local actors influenced the experiences described in the narratives. The commitment to change is related to the power that a person or group has to generate change.

Assets-based stones: For example, to understand women's relationship to different resources (stones) in terms of two related dimensions: access to (x-axis) and control over (y-axis).

Design recommendations

The same recommendations for designing sliders and sliders with stones apply to the design of a canvas with stones. In addition:

- Background image and element labels are best kept clear and simple, due to technical limitations and for easy visualization.
- As the respondent is being asked to think about the relationship between two aspects of a concept (represented along the X and Y axes), the two dimensions should be interrelated.
- There should not be more than two questions of this type in a single signification framework, as they take time and skills to facilitate well, and require considerable effort from the respondent.
- It is advisable to list few options: these questions take time to facilitate and respondents need to reflect more, and if many, respondents' fatigue can be expected.
- Devices that run iOS have proven more reliable and easier to use than Android devices, which can fail to properly display more than five response options to these question type.

Data format generated

Pattern visualization for each issue (stone).
Quantitative data are captured for the X and Y coordinates, generating a value that ranges from 0 to 100 from left to right for the X coordinate; and from 0 to 100 from bottom to top for the Y coordinate.

Table 15. Examples of canvas-with-stones signifier questions

Issue-based stones

In the experience you shared, how do you see the natural resources in your land?

1. Water before the experience
2. Water now
3. Soil before the experience
4. Soil now

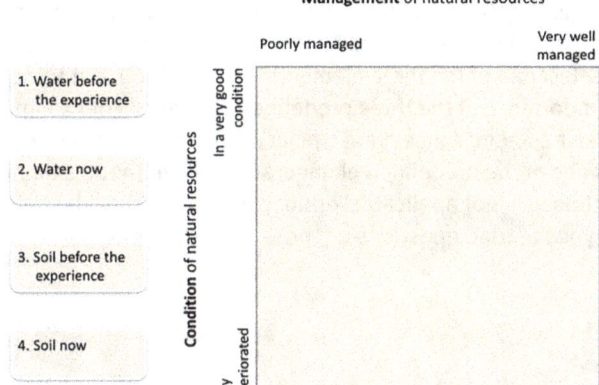

Actor-based stones

In the story you shared, the following actors have the…

1. Peace and order Committee
2. Municipal leaders
3. Military / police
4. Traditional / religious leaders
5. Community

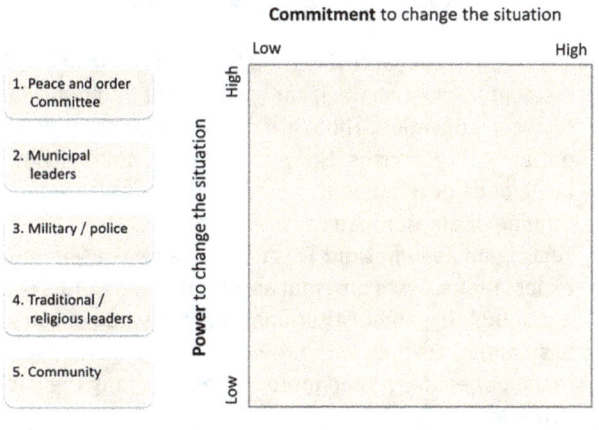

Assets-based stones

In the experience you shared, when attempting to improve your food production and/or income in relation to…

1. Plot of personal land
2. Money
3. Time and labor
4. Equipment and tools

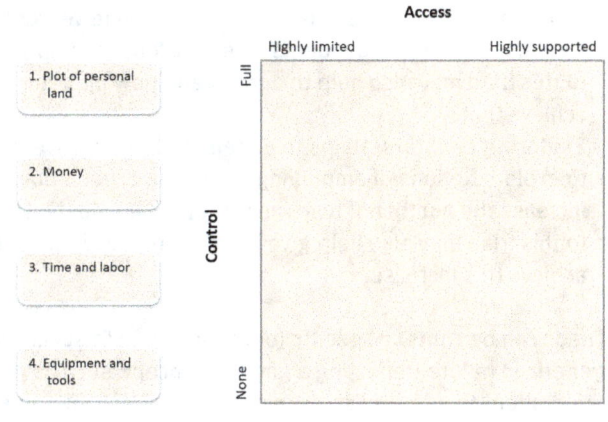

Designing triad signifier questions

A triad question is an equilateral triangle with element labels on the corners. It aims to determine the relative importance of three different elements of a single concept in the experience shared by the respondent. Respondents are not asked to select one of the three elements, as in an MCQ, but rather to indicate the relative importance of the three predefined elements. For example, the elements of the 'self-esteem' concept are 'social connections', 'knowledge/skills' and 'confidence'. If none of the predefined elements is relevant to the experience, the respondent may choose a 'not applicable' option, which also provides valuable information. Several types of triad questions are possible (see Tables 16 and 17 for examples).

Table 16. Variations, design recommendations, and data format generated for triad questions

Variations of triad questions

Triads can be classified by their main purpose.

- **Exploring a concept:** This triad type explores the relative strength of the three elements. For example, it can give insight into behavioral changes resulting from financial education. There are no assumptions and no expectations of specific patterns of responses. However, from the point of view of a program that supports livelihoods development, it would be desirable for more savings to be used for farming or entrepreneurial activities.
- **Testing an assumption:** This triad type tests assumptions, theories, or expectations. Tests program assumptions, theories or expectations. For example, about building and institutionalizing the value of conservation. One of the assumptions is that, with time, interventions will contribute to fewer responses in the upper corner, and more responses along the line between the two lower corners.
- **Exploring constraints:** Helps to understand the relative importance of constraints and how to dampen them; all three elements of the triad are negative. The expectation is that interventions will result in fewer responses that fall inside the shape, with more respondents selecting 'does not apply'. Analyzing responses to this triad may also help to understand how interventions can be adjusted to achieve that.
- **Exploring enablers:** Helps to understand the relative importance of enablers and to explore options of amplifying them. The expectation is that interventions will increase the number of responses that fall inside the shape. Analyzing responses to this triad may also help give insight into how interventions can be adjusted to achieve this increase.

Triads can be **context-specific** (only applicable to specific project or study) or more **generic** in nature (reflecting a general concept, such as power, identity, or temporal orientation) that is applicable in multiple projects or studies.

Design recommendations

- The selection or identification of the triad elements could be informed by the analytical framing of the study. Each triad reflects a concept that the study seeks to help understand.
- The three items that shape the corners of a triad should be carefully chosen as elements of the same concept, so they are interrelated and can therefore blend.
- None of the elements should be mutually exclusive (e.g. for the concept of decision-making in a household, one should not use 'only myself', 'only my partner' and 'only other household members'). Mutually exclusive options are better in the form of an MCQ.
- The three elements should be all positive, all negative, or all neutral. Avoid mixing positive and negative elements in a single triad.
- Drafting the signification framework is a creative process that often results in many triad questions. If this is the case, the team must critically assess and prioritize the questions. It is best not to include more than six triads in the signification framework, as they must be well facilitated and may be difficult to respond to.

Data format generated

Quantitative data, with each response captured in two ways:

- as X and Y coordinates that enable the dots to be plotted in the triangle, and
- as ratios of the distances to each of the three corners (each of the elements in the concept being explored), from 0 to 100, with a total height of 100 percent. The closer the response to the element (corner), the higher the value of this element is.

There are different variations on each question type. The way triads are constructed depends partly on their purpose: they can be used to explore or understand a particular concept through the lens of three elements that compose this concept. For example, the concept of 'justice' can be seen as restitution, retribution, or revenge. The three elements are equally possible ways to seek 'justice'; there is no preferred situation, answer, or expectation embedded in these elements. In the example shown in Table 17, the aim is to explore whether project participants have internalized saving as a behavioral change and, if so, how they are using their savings; again, there is no preferred situation. Other triads are used to evaluate three elements and test a specific assumption. A particular answer pattern indicates the confirmation of an assumption or the effect of an intervention. A third purpose is related to understanding constraints and enablers of particular situations, generating insights into their nature. This indicates their presence in relation to the situation described in the narratives. Examples of these are provided in Table 17.

Triads can vary in terms of specificity (see Table 18). Some are only applicable to a specific context; these are tailor-made and more detailed. Others are more generic, as they consider dimensions of a concept that are relevant in different settings or for different topics.

A Practical Guide for Using SenseMaker

Table 17. Examples of triad signifier questions by purpose

Exploring a concept
In the experience you shared, you used more of your savings to...

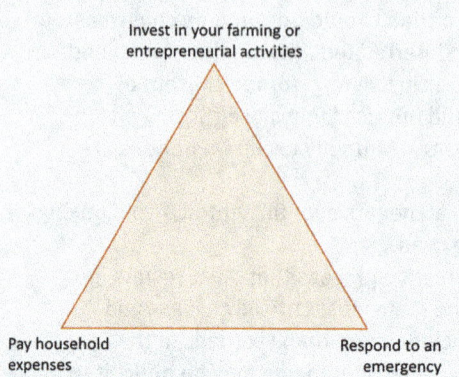

Testing an assumption
In the experience you have just shared, the following make it difficult to overcome and recuperate...

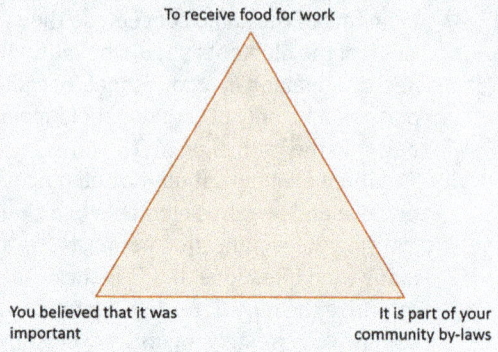

Exploring constraints
In the experience you have just shared, the following make it difficult to overcome and recuperate...

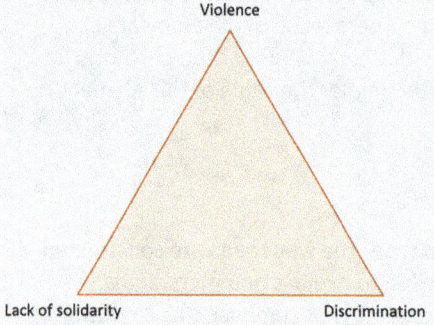

Exploring enablers
Did you experience any of the following? If so, what helped you to overcome the experience shared?

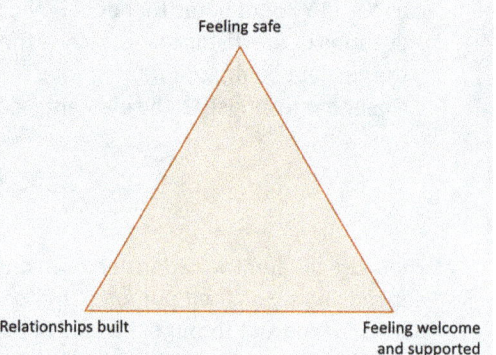

Table 18. Examples of context-specific versus generic triad signifier questions

Context-specific triad
In your story, the farmers ...

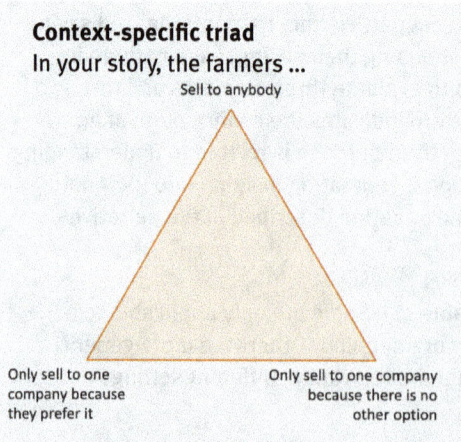

Generic triad
In your story, people ...

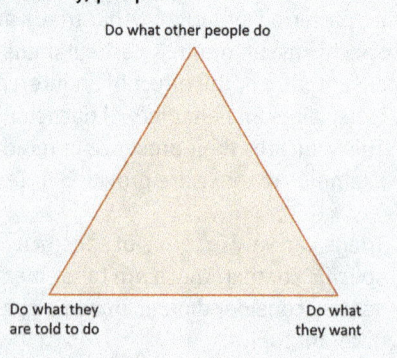

Context-specific triad
This triad was designed to give insight into the perceptions of the loyalty or dependency of farmer organizations on their buyers. This is a context-specific triad that will only be used in studies about farmers' collective marketing experiences.

Generic triad
This triad was designed to give insight into how people act in any situation described in their story. This generic triad can be used in many studies, even if narratives are generated with very different prompters.

Step 4: Drafting signifier and sociodemographic MCQs

Multiple-choice questions (MCQs) are not unique to SenseMaker. However, it is important to understand how they are used in the SenseMaker context. When MCQs relate to the narrative, they function as signifier questions, but when they relate to the respondent, they are sociodemographic MCQs. Examples of signifier MCQs are presented in Table 19. These two types of MCQs are critical for analytical and visualization purposes, as they enable color coding of the visual patterns.

Signifier MCQs about the narratives are essential, as they help understand more about the narrative as perceived by the respondent. Since the narrative text does not usually contain all the information about the specific experience, signifier MCQs help to capture these nuances, thus providing additional layers of information about the nature of the story. For example, they may ask how the respondent feels about their experience, which issues or people were important or influential, what the experience was about, when it took place, or how frequently these types of experience happen. MCQs help to disaggregate the narratives to allow comparison of textual information by theme and by subgroup.

Sociodemographic MCQs about respondents are also essential in any signification framework. Such questions allow disaggregation of findings and therefore the assessment of differences between subsets of respondents. For example, they can show how respondents who feel positive about their experiences differ from those who feel negative about them. They allow the SenseMaker team to:

- ensure there is the right proportion for each subgroup of interest (for representative sampling);
- identify dominant and less represented subsets of the sample data, which is important for making valid generalizations;
- disaggregate findings in order to assess the differences between subsets of respondents, for example by comparing responses by gender or geography; and
- contextualize and interpret findings.

Respondents answer MCQs by selecting one or multiple responses from a predefined list. Some examples of signifier MCQs are presented in Table 19.

Table 19. Design recommendations and data format generated for multiple-choice questions

Design recommendations

- Where possible, it is recommended to have as few response options as possible, without compromising the value during the sensemaking phase.
- The 'not applicable' option is used to allow respondents to not respond to a question that does not apply to the experience shared, or to simply opt out of responding. There are instances in which this should be used.
- The free-text 'other' box option is often included when there is a sense that respondents may provide additional and valuable information beyond the predefined options of the MCQs. Analysis of this free text data, however, may be complicated, and may require a post-categorization process.
- MCQs that allow more than one answer require extra work in preparing the data set and slightly complicate the sensemaking process. It is recommended that the number of MCQs are limited.
- Clearly state if the respondent must select only one response or may select multiple responses. The exact minimum or maximum number of responses to be selected in multiple response MCQs can also be specified.

Data format generated

- Pattern visualization
- Quantitative data are captured with a value of 1 if the respondent selects the given choice.
- Textual data are generated by the 'other' free text response option, if applicable.

Table 20. Examples of signifier MCQs

How do you feel now about the experience you shared?
(Select only one response)

- ❏ Positive
- ❏ Neutral
- ❏ Negative

The experience you shared made you feel... *(Select up to two responses)*

- ❏ Proud
- ❏ Happy
- ❏ Hopeful
- ❏ Indifferent
- ❏ Frustrated / Angry
- ❏ Sad
- ❏ Worried
- ❏ Other (please specify)_____

The experience you shared is about... *(Select as many responses as apply)*

- ❏ Friendship
- ❏ Education
- ❏ Marriage
- ❏ Safety / Security
- ❏ Freedom to move around
- ❏ Health
- ❏ Violence
- ❏ Family relationships
- ❏ Household chores
- ❏ A romantic relationship
- ❏ A girl's honor
- ❏ Menstruation
- ❏ Dowry
- ❏ Income
- ❏ Other (please specify)_____

Who was most helpful in helping you to recover from the challenging event in the experience you shared? *(Select only one response)*

- ❏ Family / Relatives
- ❏ Neighbors / Friends
- ❏ Religious group
- ❏ Community organization
- ❏ Government organization
- ❏ Project-implementing NGO
- ❏ Other NGOs
- ❏ Other (please specify)_____

When did the experience you shared take place? *(Select only one response)*

- ❏ In the last year
- ❏ 1-2 years ago
- ❏ More than 3 years ago

How often do experiences similar to what you described happen?
(Select only one response)

- ❏ Never, this was the first time
- ❏ Rarely
- ❏ Sometimes
- ❏ Often
- ❏ All the time

A Practical Guide for Using SenseMaker

Step 5: Questions to obtain respondents' consent to share the narrative

Ethically, it is essential to ask permission from storytellers to document their story and to use the data for analysis purposes. However, personal stories can also be used in debriefing sessions, collective interpretation workshops, publications, or communications to the wider public (e.g. websites, public dashboards, briefings). Storytellers thus need the opportunity to explicitly give or refuse their permission for their story to be used in the public domain.

Testing and Critically Reviewing the Signification Framework

A newly designed signification framework usually requires a few rounds of testing, such as preliminary testing (resulting in the first critical review of the signification framework), in-situ testing (resulting in the second critical review), and user testing (resulting in the final review; Figure 9). In cases where an existing signification framework is being adapted, it is still recommended that a critical review and a final user testing be organized. For replication, user testing is usually sufficient.

Signification framework tests and reviews

First critical review. After the first draft of the framework has been designed, it needs to be tested, critically reviewed, and revised. Ideally, testing should be conducted by a SenseMaker-trained design team with in-depth knowledge of the analytical framework underpinning the design and active involvement in drafting the signification framework. Critical review of the draft signification framework involves testing and revising all questions.

Second critical review. This review involves in-situ testing in the context in which collection will take place. Once the first draft of the signification framework has been developed and tested by the design team, it should be reviewed again. At this stage, it is very useful to involve people who are not part of the design team — including potential respondents, analysts (project or partner organization staff), and thematic experts (e.g. disaster relief or gender experts) — as well as some program participants, if the application focuses on a program. During this in-situ testing, the translation of the framework into the collection language may not have been finalized. In this case, the testing may coincide with simultaneous translation. This will not provide insights about the clarity of questions or their wording, but it will give an idea of whether the questions make sense to respondents and whether the length of the framework is appropriate.

Final review. This round of testing is undertaken by the facilitators as part of their training, with a full draft in the language of collection. It assesses how the framework is understood by respondents and whether the digital version for collection through the app is functional, suitable, and user-friendly. The test outcomes are then systematically recorded and reviewed, and the paper and digital versions of the framework are revised.

What needs to be reviewed

While all testing and review processes should look at multiple aspects of the signification framework and collection, the main focus of each review depends on the stage of the design process (Figure 10).

Ensure question design quality. All questions should be well developed and follow the recommendations provided in Step 3: Drafting core SenseMaker signifier questions. Even if the questions are conceptually well-designed, it is nonetheless important to test how the respondents answer them. For example, are there too many 'not applicable' responses? Does everyone tend to respond in the same way? Identify gaps. It is important to ensure that all required concepts, contexts, and sociodemographic characteristics are included in the signification framework, and that when combined they respond to learning questions.

Prioritize questions. Testing helps to identify and reduce duplication and to prioritize the follow-up signifier questions and sociodemographic MCQs. Prioritizing is about making sure that only those questions in the framework that are relevant, add most value, and serve the intended purpose are included.

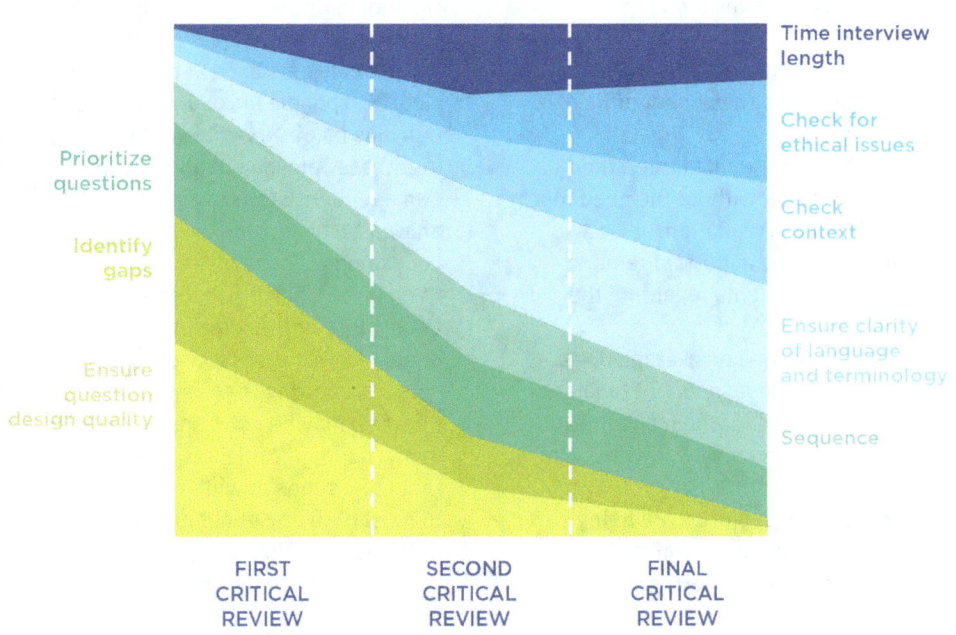

Figure 10. Changing the review focus at different stages of the signification framework design

Sequence. Ensure that smooth conversation can be carried out with respondents, minimizing jumping between topics and reducing the effort needed for responses. Sensitive questions should not be placed early on. Ensure clarity of language and terminology. The language of the signification framework should be clear and unambiguous. Respondents should not have any difficulties in understanding the instructions, questions, or response options. This is especially important for processes where collection will take place in a language other than that used by the design team. In this case, it is important to ensure that the intended meaning of questions and response options is not altered during translation.

Check context. Check the questions to ensure that assumptions about the context correctly reflect the reality, for example, program assumptions about the main source of income or the distances refugees travel daily.

Check for ethical issues. Ensure the framework is ethical in terms of collection approach, question wording, and response options.

Box 8. Checklist of questions for testing a draft signification framework

FOR THE PROMPTER

- Is the question clear?
- Does it generate relevant, informative, factual narratives?
- Are the narratives all positive or all negative?
- Are the narratives too long or too short?
- Does the title question confuse people, or do they find it difficult to respond to?
- Do the respondents understand the prompter without the need for additional explanation?
- Are there any important remarks from respondents regarding the prompters?
- How much time on average does it take for the respondent to share the story, and for the facilitator to document and review it with the respondent?
- What kinds of stories are being generated by the prompter? Are they the type of stories expected?

FOR TRIAD, SLIDER, SLIDER-WITH-STONES, AND CANVAS-WITH-STONES QUESTIONS

- Is the language clear?
- Are the questions in a meaningful order?
- Is there survey fatigue? Do the respondents get tired too quickly?
- Do people understand each question without too much explanation?
- Are the concepts used in the questions clear? Do people make a deliberate choice?
- Can bias be observed toward the obvious 'right' answer when people respond?
- Can a tendency toward a particular answer be observed, such as for triads? For example: Too many responses in the middle, showing that the relative importance of the three elements is equal? Too many responses in one or more corners, showing that a multiple-choice question may be more appropriate? Too many 'not applicable' responses, showing that the options provided are not relevant to most of the respondents? Are the patterns visualized using the test data meaningful and relevant?

Time interview length. Ensure that the interview length is feasible for the program and for respondents, being short enough to avoid fatigue, which can compromise data quality.

Box 8 provides examples of the questions that can be used to guide the signification framework testing and review processes during all stages of revising.

Documenting the testing and review process

The testing process should be documented properly, as it is usually conducted by different members of the design team at different times. It will be helpful for the design team, and particularly for the person responsible for producing the final draft, to have all the observations, suggestions, and major inputs for every revision of the signification framework in a single document leading to the final draft, or to save every draft separately so as to have a record of historic changes.

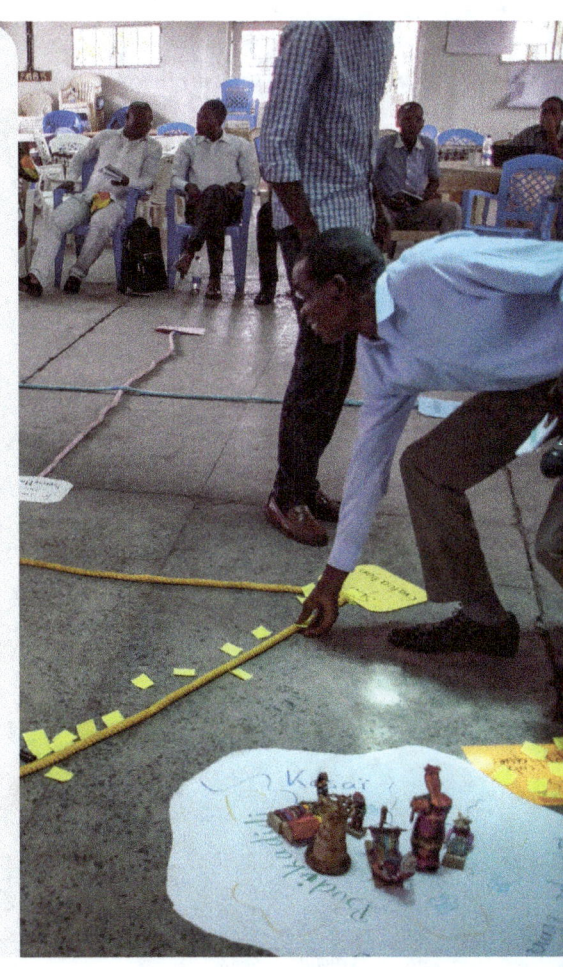

FOR MULTIPLE-CHOICE QUESTIONS

- Are all the answer options presented clearly and understood by the respondents?
- Are there questions that allow a free text response? If so, is it absolutely necessary? What responses are you expecting, and can any response be added to existing responses? Or are you expecting to do post-categorization based on responses to a free text field?
- Is there a tendency to select only one or two answer options from the list? Why?
- Have all possible responses been considered for sociodemographic questions?

GENERAL

- Are there any ethical issues with the prompter or with any of the signifier or multiple-choice questions?
- Does the signification framework have a logical flow, or do signifier questions need to be rearranged?

Creating and Testing the Digital Version of the Signification Framework

Once the final draft of the signification framework has been produced, the next step is to configure it digitally. This configuration can be completely new or can be based on an existing framework that is adapted. Digital configuration can be carried out using the Designer[2] functionality or a third-party survey tool, such as SurveyCTO.[3] Once the framework configuration has been completed, the instrument can be accessed digitally through an application on a device (tablet or phone) or a browser via a URL.

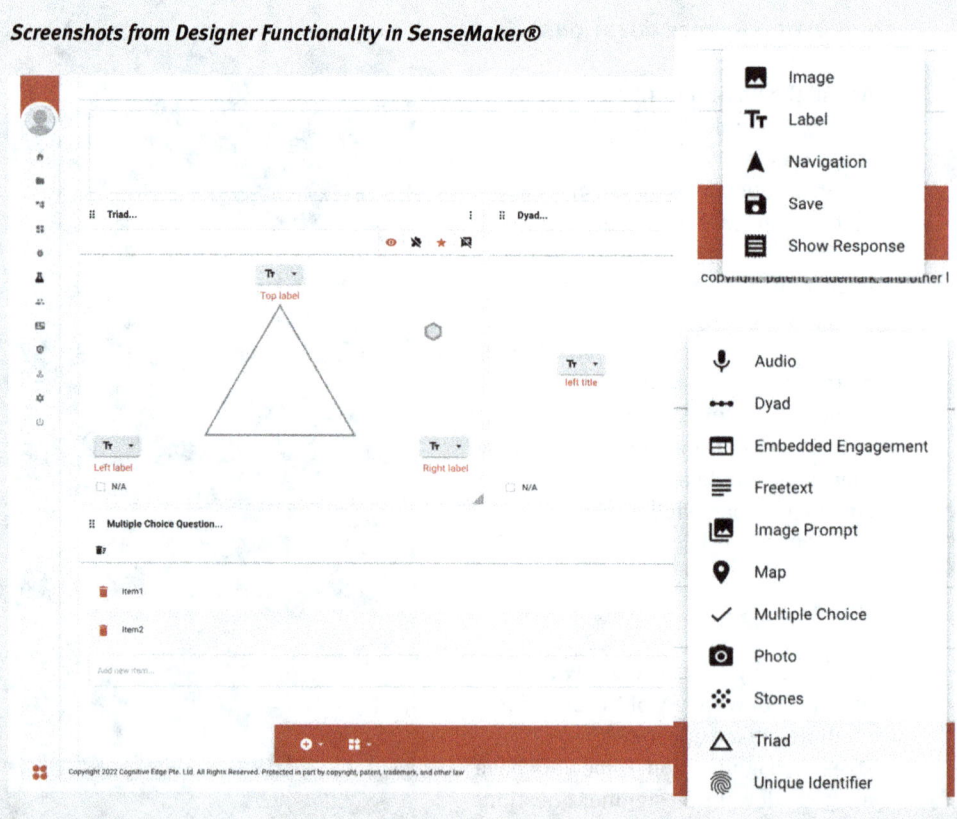

Screenshots from Designer Functionality in SenseMaker®

2. Configuration in Designer requires a license and training and help from an expert user.
3. The use of third party survey tools for digital framework configuration and data collection must be agreed with The Cynefin Company.

Translating the Signification Framework

If the collection is to be undertaken in a language other than that used by the design team, the signification framework should be translated by a fluent speaker, and ideally by someone who also has technical knowledge of the topic and its terminology. Translation begins after the signification framework has been tested and the language has been finalized.

During the translation process, ensure that back-translation is used to verify that the terms reflect their intended meaning, rather than just a literal translation. Preparing a glossary of key terms and agreeing on them with the design team will be very useful during this process. The final user testing, which is conducted during the training of facilitators (see Phase 3: Collection), is fundamental to testing the translation and making final adjustments.

Phase 3: Collection

- 93 Collection Scenarios
- 94 Collection Principles
- 96 Ethics during the Collection Process
- 97 How to Collect Data Step-by-Step
- 97 Step 1: Preparing for Collection
- 104 Step 2: Training Facilitators and Conducting Final User Testing
- 107 Step 3: Facilitating the Collection Process
- 118 Step 4: Monitoring Collection and Ensuring Data Quality

The collection process is a time for listening, allowing people to share their specific experiences and to provide additional layers of information about their experiences, the emotions they bring about, the process of change, the outcomes of the experience, and any other aspects that arise as they reflect.

Phase 3: Collection

The collection process is a time for listening, allowing people to share their specific experiences and to provide additional layers of information about their experiences, the emotions they bring about, the process of change, the outcomes of the experience, and any other aspects that arise as they reflect. This additional information is provided by respondents when they answer the follow-up questions. The process involves using the signification framework to facilitate conversations with respondents and to allow their self-reflection, yielding qualitative and quantitative data. The quality of the data generated is the foundation for useful analysis and interpretation, and for robust and credible findings that can lead to better decisions and needed actions.

Collection Scenarios

Depending on the level of literacy of respondents and their access to the internet, as well as on the context, data can be collected in four ways:

- facilitated individually face-to-face,
- facilitated individually remotely,
- facilitated in group settings, and
- through direct distribution of the signification framework to respondents (sharing of URL).

The first three involve one-to-one (face-to-face or remote) or group facilitating conversations with the respondents, with answers entered into devices or written on paper copies of the framework. Direct distribution of the framework involves providing a URL to the respondents, which allows access to the digitally configured signification framework, letting them answer the questions on their own, though often within a specified time frame.

Individual face-to-face facilitation will be described in more detail, as it requires consideration of varying levels of literacy. Data can be collected through an app, through a browser, on paper, or any combination of these.

Collection scenarios may vary depending on the purpose of the SenseMaker project. If it is used for frequent monitoring, collection can be integrated into daily work of staff. When a baseline, assessment, evaluation, or study is planned, the timing for collection is precisely defined, with all data usually collected in two to four weeks.

Collection Principles

Principle 1.
Design a collection approach that is appropriate to the specific context.

There is no one-size-fits-all approach for collecting. Collection will depend on many factors in each context, including respondents' literacy levels, access to the internet, security issues, and social and cultural norms.

Principle 2.
Ensure an ethical collection process that protects respondents.

The well-being and safety of respondents and facilitators come first. A 'do no harm' approach is essential during the entire collection phase. It must be part of facilitator training.

Principle 3.
Provide quality training to facilitators and ensure sufficient practice.

One of the most important activities during the collection phase is the selection and training of facilitators. SenseMaker requires collecting a good quality narrative and facilitating a reflection process that allows respondents to self-interpret the experience shared. This means facilitators must be able to build rapport with the respondent and use good listening skills to facilitate and document the process.

Principle 4.
Conduct a final user-test with facilitators.

Once facilitators are well-trained, they can be knowledgeable signification framework testers. Their familiarity with the collection context can be an invaluable contribution to perfect the signification framework design, with words easily understood by respondents. This final user testing of the framework is usually conducted as part of the training, leading to the final revisions in paper and digital versions.

Principle 5.
Encourage facilitators to listen and facilitate reflection by respondents.

Deep, factual and empathic listening is required to capture the narrative. The role of the facilitator is to encourage the sharing of a meaningful experience and to guide respondents through their self-signification process, without intervening or intermediating with their own assumptions, but rather respecting respondents' perceptions and perspectives.

Principle 6.
Provide facilitators with written instructions to follow during the collection process.

Good instructions to facilitate the collection process are fundamental. Preparing a facilitation manual for the facilitators can help ensure high quality data and respectful collection processes. Part of such a manual is generic for facilitating collection, with another part focused on the signification framework. If the objective is to collect complete and well-written narratives that will allow text analysis, these instructions may include a protocol for the collection of the narratives that include follow-up questions to elicit a good narrative, such as what happened, who was involved, how did it happen, what were the outcomes (positive or negative)?

Principle 7.
Use practical exercises to facilitate the collection process.

Using practical exercises in open spaces when one-to-one and face-to-face facilitation is used makes it easier for respondents (especially those with lower literacy) to understand how to respond thoughtfully to triads, sliders, and canvas questions. Such exercises are recommended when the respondent has never been asked these question types before and can keep them engaged in the process.

Principle 8.
Monitor the collection process closely.

Detailed daily follow-up, particularly during the first days, can help identify challenges in the quality of narratives, facilitation of signifier questions, and technical issues. The earlier that problems can be identified and addressed, the more likely that ethical problems can be avoided and the better the data that will be collected.

Ethics During the Collection Process

During collection, direct interaction with participants takes place. Ethical practices are the cornerstone of safe collection, with doing no harm a critical and basic standard. The safety of facilitators must be considered as much as that of respondents.

Making sure no harm happens to respondents, with benefits of the research outweighing any risks, means that facilitators need to be able to manage respondents' emotions and to deal with unexpected challenges during collection. This is particularly important when working with vulnerable respondents or exploring sensitive topics. Some groups of respondents, such as refugees, may have been exposed to violence, threats, or stigma. A sensitive interviewing approach is paramount. It is not possible to anticipate what respondents will be sharing in their narratives. Doing no harm means being able to sensitively steer the conversation back to the questions in the signification framework.

Issues for which respondents need support may emerge during interviews. Facilitators should prepare themselves with information so they can refer people to specialized organizations that can handle such cases. The organization in charge of the process should provide facilitators with their own protocols. Figure 11 gives an overview of how ethics are embedded throughout the process, with particular importance during the Collection phase.

Explicit consent is required from respondents for three aspects of collection: general participation in the study, audio recording, and sharing narratives. It should also be stated explicitly at the outset that the respondent has the right to halt the process at any point, without any negative consequences or questions.

Figure 11. When to consider ethics (adapted from Oxfam, 2020)

Design	Conduct risk analysis	Select participants	Gain consent	Conduct interview	Use findings
Reduce risks and increase benefit for participants	Identify risks	Ensure benefit for participants	Ensure informed & voluntary consent (for children from guardians)	Train facilitators	Explain how findings will be used
Protect vulnerable participants	Develop risk mitigation strategy	Ensure greater benefits than risks	Carefully gain consent from vulnerable groups	Ensure safety and comfort for everyone	Participants choose if and how they are identified
Ensure that questions are respectful and culturally appropriate	Monitor risks throughout	Select well to limit bias	Never force participation	Report any serious adverse effects of participation	Record their choices
				Ensure participants can contact facilitators	Protect anonymity

Confidentiality is also essential. Responses remain confidential when any identifying personal information is known only to the research team. Confidentiality is ensured by separating data from identifying information and storing the data securely. It also means restricting access to raw data to the SenseMaker project team and other authorized individuals who will maintain confidentiality. This may mean anonymizing data and findings by omitting personal identifying information.

Facilitators need to have specific guidelines, for example, referral and counter-referral protocols in cases of gender-based violence or abuse, and practical recommendations on how to implement the organization's code of conduct. If ethical review board approval is required, it must be obtained after the signification framework is designed, and before beginning the collection process.

How to Collect Data Step-by-Step

The four steps of the Collection phase are:

Step 1: Preparing for collection.
Step 2: Training facilitators and conducting final user testing.
Step 3: Facilitating the collection process through
- individual face-to-face facilitation,
- individual remote facilitation,
- facilitation in group settings, or
- direct distribution of the signification framework.

Step 4: Monitoring the collection process and ensuring data quality

The guidance given here assumes that data are collected in facilitated, face-to-face interactions, and can be adapted for facilitated, remote interaction. If collection proceeded through direct distribution of the signification frameworks online, then Step 1 will be different and Step 2 will be omitted. However, it is advisable to include in the design an explanation on how to respond to the SenseMaker-specific signifier questions, including some simple practice exercises. This will help respondents to understand the questions, and therefore, provide accurate responses.

Step 1: Preparing for Collection

Many aspects of the collection logistics will have been decided and prepared during the Preparation and Design phases. At this stage, ensure that all preparations have been finalized, and revisit the original plan to make any changes needed.

Communicate with stakeholders. A final check is advised to confirm that local partners and other stakeholders who are involved or important for smooth collection are fully informed about the precise plans and expectations for collection. They will have been contacted and engaged with during the Preparation phase. In some contexts, it may be mandatory to ask community and religious leaders and the household head for permission to collect. At this stage, it is about confirming agreed plans: dates, locations, numbers of respondents per day, roles and responsibilities. Plans usually need some adaptation due to the inevitable dynamics of any context.

Prepare and test the design and collection platform. Review the digital version of the signification framework to ensure that the formatting and all questions display correctly by comparing with the paper version. Once the formatting has been verified and all the final improvements have been made in the digital version of the signification framework, the next step is to enter and upload dummy responses. Check whether all test observations are present and displaying correctly in the dataset, and whether all the variables are displaying as expected with their exact titles.

If devices are used for collection, they will have been procured during the Preparation phase. The data collection app needs to be installed on each device and the signification framework should be downloaded. Once the collection process starts, and especially during the first days, it is essential that a team member is responsible for monitoring the responses uploaded online daily in order to verify that all the entries are uploading properly, to ensure the quality of the collected data, and to identify any technical difficulties early on.

Prepare all training and collection materials and handouts. Allow adequate time to prepare training materials, including flipcharts, handouts, and exercises. Translations of the signification framework and other training material, including the draft facilitator manual, will also be needed. It is essential that there are sufficient copies of the paper version of the signification framework for each facilitator and for the final user testing. It is also good practice to have the signification framework printed as flipcharts and displayed on a wall throughout the training event. If the data are to be collected using devices, they need to be procured and have the collection app installed and the signification framework downloaded. This allows facilitators to be trained in their use and to practice during the workshop and as part of final user testing.

Finalize logistics. Confirm all the logistics for the facilitator training, in-situ practice, user testing, and the actual collection. This involves transportation, accommodation, food, and security checks of the areas where collection will occur.

Planning the collection process

The time and resources needed for the collection process will depend on several considerations. These will have been discussed during the Preparation and Design phases, and should be finalized just prior to collection.

Sample size and the number of available facilitators

The use of twelve to fifteen facilitators has worked well in collecting several hundred narratives. This reduces the collection period to two or three weeks, as each facilitator can collect between three and six narratives per day, depending on how long the signification framework is and how much time it takes to move from one respondent to the next. A larger sample of respondents or widely geographically dispersed respondents will require more days of collection or more facilitators. These can be contracted if staff cannot commit to this task.

Collection approaches

Collection can happen on paper or digitally (using an app or browser), face-to-face, remote, or in group settings. The choice between paper and digital collection will depend on factors including respondent characteristics (ease and comfort with paper or electronics), device availability, budget, and the ability of facilitators to move around safely with the devices.

With greater digital connection worldwide, and the growing number of people familiar with electronic devices, digital collection is advisable. Digital collection eliminates errors caused by transcription, stores data more securely, stores data directly online, makes data quality assurance easier, and enables primary analysis to begin as soon as the collection process ends. If collection is to be paper-based, extra time for transcribing narratives and entering the responses via an app or a browser needs to be planned and budgeted for.

Length of the signification framework

The longer the signification framework and the more core SenseMaker questions it contains, the longer each interview will take. The time needed will also depend on the collection tool used (whether digital or paper) and on respondents' comfort with that tool and with the process in general. Experience shows that collection varies from 20 minutes to two hours. The longer a session lasts, the more effort is needed by everyone involved, and the quality of the data may be negatively affected.

Keeping track of how long it takes to conduct interviews under real collection conditions is important. This will help ensure that the facilitation process is manageable for respondents and facilitators. Facilitators will also be able to give respondents a clearer estimate of how much time is being asked of them.
It is important to keep in mind that working with sensitive topics—such as abuse, violence, social conflict, loss of assets, or the death of family members—may take longer, as facilitators and respondents may need time to process their emotions during the facilitation of the process.

Literacy level of respondents

Experience has shown that more literate respondents usually tend to grasp the different types of questions more quickly. Respondents with more limited literacy may require more consistent support during the process although this is not always the case. Facilitator training must include a discussion of the qualities and soft competencies needed for facilitating the collection process, and tips on how to explain and facilitate the more unusual SenseMaker signifier question types should be provided. If respondents are sufficiently literate, a group-based collection process becomes an option. In this, one facilitator works with multiple respondents simultaneously, seated in a group, working through each question as they respond individually on devices or on paper.

Direct distribution of the signification framework for respondents to fill their responses themselves with no facilitation is more appropriate for more literate respondents. Nevertheless, it is essential to include clear explanations on how to respond to the SenseMaker-specific signifier questions as even more literate respondents are unlikely to be familiar with these types of questions. In addition, some simple practice exercises can also be included prior to the first question of each type.

Possible security issues for respondents and facilitators

Some SenseMaker processes take place in areas where the security of respondents and facilitators needs special attention—notably in natural disaster zones and in areas where there is civil unrest. In one case, for example, facilitators were threatened, with their devices temporarily confiscated by local youths, before being returned after some negotiation (Guijt and Mager 2017). Daily security briefings were held to determine which areas were safe for collection. In other countries, devices have been stolen, putting the lives of facilitators at risk. A security risk assessment may lead to the decision to conduct the collection process on paper to reduce the risk to facilitators. Security issues should thus be planned for, with alternative plans for collection being identified ahead of time.

Finding, selecting, and contracting facilitators

An important task in preparing for the collection process is to identify a good team of facilitators. Facilitators can be local volunteers or peers, staff of organizations involved in development efforts, staff of other organizations (such as think tanks), university students, freelance consultants or consultancy firms, or research organizations. Regardless of their background, it is essential for facilitators to have a minimum set of competencies to facilitate the process in an ethical manner, to ensure good rapport with respondents, and to guarantee the quality of the narratives and responses collected.

If SenseMaker is being used for evaluation purposes, involving staff of the initiative being evaluated should be considered with caution, as they can potentially bias responses. On the other hand, involving program implementation staff in a diagnostic or assessment study to inform program design or adaptation, proved to be a great opportunity for them to engage directly with program participants to better understand their needs, emergent practices, and the implementation context. Working with survey companies also has potential drawbacks. Enumerators will need to learn a more facilitation-type approach. Becoming facilitators will require unlearning survey habits, making training, coaching, and supervision essential. This drawback can be reduced by making explicit in the Terms of Reference that SenseMaker will be used, with a clear explanation of the method and its specific collection needs. Once the contractor is selected, a series of meetings with an experienced SenseMaker practitioner can give the contractor a good understanding of the method and its special needs. If this is the first time that the contractor will undertake collection using SenseMaker, time from an experienced SenseMaker practitioner for training purposes is vital.

Training is easier when facilitators have a higher level of education. Across different SenseMaker processes, there have been good experiences with students from local universities, high-school graduates, and also with peers. Their level of education, commitment, and eagerness to learn and acquire practical experience makes them excellent facilitators. In certain contexts, peers are better accepted than external people. Facilitators should expect that participating in the training and in-situ practice is a mandatory part of the collection process.

When selecting facilitators, consider these aspects in particular:

- **Language:** Fluency in the language of collection is essential. Often, they should be able to master the local and the collection language.
- **Gender:** The specific gender mix of facilitators may matter depending on the topic of inquiry. For example, female facilitators may be needed when interviewing girls on topics that are culturally sensitive. In other cases, male facilitators may be more appropriate.
- **Age:** In some contexts, respondents were more willing to share personal stories with mature people than with youths.
- **Culture and social identity:** Facilitators should have knowledge of the local context and what is culturally appropriate. For example, if working with special groups, such as relatives of prisoners who are stigmatized, facilitators need the confidence and skills to cope with this.
- **Basic professional qualities:** The ability to work in a team, to meet deadlines, to be prepared to speak up if issues on the ground threaten work quality, to follow security and ethic protocols, and to be respectful.
- **Social and emotional competencies:** Capacity to listen and communicate effectively, to create rapport with respondents, empathize, and be culturally sensitive.
- **Curiosity and creativity:** Some facilitation competencies will be built or strengthened during training, including technical and methodological competencies. However, what is not easily taught is being open-minded to new ways of knowing. If possible, select facilitators who are curious and open to new approaches and methods, and able and willing to unlearn old ways of data collection.

Preparing the electronic devices for collection

The devices for collection will have been procured and tested. Several tasks need to be undertaken for each device before they are ready for use (see Box 9).

Organizing logistics for facilitator training and the final user test

Facilitator training and the final user testing of the signification framework require carefully planning. Here are some important considerations; these are not exhaustive, and others may be needed. Table 21 provides a list of what to check before the collection preparation process is wrapped up.

Box 9. Tasks to prepare devices for collection

- Clean the devices.
- Delete videos, photos, and other large files to free up memory.
- Ensure that each device has a charger.
- Update the operating system software (iOS for iPads).
- Ensure that location services are on.
- Ensure that each device has its passcode.
- Install the SenseMaker Collector app from the Play Store (Android) or the App Store (iOS).
- Download the final version of the signification framework to the device using the Project ID. Then ensure no changes have been made in Designer.
- Ensure that the time before the devices go into 'sleep mode' is longer than the time it takes to collect the narrative. Usually ten minutes will be enough, but if a more complete narrative is expected, it may take longer.
- If data collection takes place in a language with special characters, download the collection language to the devices and set them up for use.
- Prepare copies of a handout that describes how to use and take care of the devices. These are to be given to each facilitator.

Table 21. Checklist to prepare for collection

Facilitators

- Find an experienced SenseMaker trainer and facilitator.
- Confirm the availability of facilitators.
- Ensure that externally hired facilitators have received their contracts.
- If program staff are to be involved, check that they have permission to take part and can commit the time needed.
- If collection will be facilitated by volunteers, ensure they are committed and available.
- Make sure there are enough facilitators for the number of narratives to be collected within the planned time frame.

Facilitator training and final user testing

- Organize a training venue with enough floor space and some free walls for flipcharts.
- Prepare a facilitator's guide with two sections: (1) general guidance that can be used for any SenseMaker process, dealing with SenseMaker in general and its different types of questions; and (2) specific instructions for the particular SenseMaker process, the collection context, and the specific signification framework.
- Invite a group of respondents to participate in the final user testing; provide them with enough information about the purpose of the activity.
- Procure any material needed: stationery, devices, ID cards for facilitators, copies of handouts, manuals, signification framework flipcharts, and paper versions for final user testing.
- Arrange meals, refreshments, accommodation, and transportation for participants.

Information

- Provide each facilitator with a handout that includes the collection schedule, the respondents assigned to them (along with alternatives, in case they cannot find the respondents according to the agreed sample method) and any other information they might need, such as facilitator and respondent IDs.

- Ensure facilitators are fully informed about ethics and sign the code of conduct.

Facilitating the collection

- Download the app and signification framework.
- Provide each facilitator with a device, charger, power bank or solar panel backpack, where necessary.
- Provide facilitators with a handout that describes how to use and take care of the device.

- Check internet connectivity in the area and provide facilitators with a modem or other options that will allow them to upload the collected data as frequently as possible.

Materials

Even if collection will be digital, provide facilitators with paper copies of the signification framework, in case of issues with the device. Give each facilitator a copy of the general facilitator's guide and the instructions manual for the specific signification framework being used. Prepare facilitation kits (for example, ropes, cards, and markers) for each facilitator. Supply each facilitator with an ID badge.

Logistics

Plan zone-based routes for facilitators that will minimize the time it takes to reach respondents. This also provides the opportunity for facilitators to support each other, exchange experiences, share challenges, and travel more safely. Each day check that all facilitators have a collection schedule and sample strategy. Ensure that facilitators have a place to recharge their devices and to access the Internet so that they can upload the narratives and responses often. Ensure that facilitators have accommodation and meals, if they are not able to return home each day.

Step 2: Training Facilitators and Conducting Final User Testing

Like any method, SenseMaker requires investment in training people who will collect data, the facilitators, to assist respondents in sharing their narratives and self-signifying them. The quality of the collected narratives and responses will largely depend on the quality of the collection process. It is, therefore, necessary to plan well and to allocate enough time for training. Experience has shown that, depending on the collection scenario and the availability of facilitators with previous SenseMaker experience, up to five days are needed, including two to three days of training, one day of practice which is also the final user testing, and one day of feedback and review of the signification framework.

The training covers the SenseMaker method, the specific signification framework designed for the process, practice of the facilitation process, and ethics during the collection process. Trainees learn how to initiate and round off the collection process and to explain core SenseMaker questions to respondents. Considerable time is often spent ensuring that facilitators are all working with the same wording of the questions and of the answer options, particularly if the language of collection differs from the language of design. Ideally, the training is conducted by an experienced SenseMaker practitioner also involved in the design process, who will have a deep knowledge and understanding of the analytical framing that informed the signification framework.

The training should include practice in the location where collection will take place. Facilitators often gain valuable insights from this, leading to final adjustments and revisions of the signification framework, and additional specific advice to add to the facilitator's manual. Several hours should be built into the schedule during, or immediately after, the training, in order to capture this feedback and revise the signification framework. These changes should then be incorporated digitally, the signification framework downloaded again onto the device, and the facilitator manual updated.

All facilitators will need to be trained in the use of the collection devices and the collection app. If collection is to be undertaken on paper, then facilitators need training in how to collect using the paper version, but also in how to enter the narratives via an app or a browser after collection.

If facilitators have previously worked as survey enumerators, they may find it difficult to let go of a more extractive and detached style of data collection. SenseMaker involves a more reflective process around the experience of the respondent. The role of the facilitator is to guide the process in a respectful, dynamic, and productive way. The way the training workshop is conducted can help facilitators see the importance of openness, patience, and active listening.

The final user testing provides a last opportunity to adjust the signification framework, especially for language use and clarity. This testing moment requires careful planning. Staff and invited participants need to be well-informed about the purpose of the sessions and the logistics.

Working with mixed methods requires additional competencies on the part of facilitators. These should be included in the profile for hiring, but they also need to be developed during training.

Objectives of facilitator training

The training workshop should equip facilitators with a good understanding of the method and the skills necessary to collect narratives, guide respondents through the self-signification process in an empathetic and ethical way, and consistently meet quality technical and methodological standards. To achieve this, the training needs to focus on strengthening four types of competencies (see Table 22).

Table 22. Facilitator competencies for collecting narratives and self-signification

	BY THE END OF THE TRAINING, FACILITATORS WILL ...
Technical competency	• Understand the basics of SenseMaker, its origins, and what makes it unique among other research, monitoring, and evaluation methods. • Understand the purpose of the SenseMaker process and the learning questions that the process aims to explore. • Understand the basic thematic focus and underlying concepts of the signification framework.
Methodological competency	• Encourage respondents to share their narrative and help them document and revise it, as needed. • Explain clearly the different types of signifier questions and facilitate the respondent's self-signification. • Facilitate the self-signification process accurately, balancing patience and efficiency, without imposing their own views. • Use digital devices and software to document the responses and upload them to the dataset.
Social & emotional competency	• Build confidence and trust with respondent, creating a safe context for sharing their narrative and self-interpretation. • Communicate with empathy so as to encourage respondents of different ages, genders, and origins, respecting the cultural context. • Act professionally and ethically, according to the organizational code of conduct and data-protection principles. • Respect respondent confidentiality when respondents have indicated they do not want their stories shared.
Change-related competency	• Accept and provide feedback, as needed, to change habits and attitudes that negatively affect the quality of the facilitation process.

Contents of training events

The contents of training events should help facilitators strengthen these competencies. Table 23 shows the basic design of a facilitator training event and how this relates to the core competencies. It can be adapted as needed. A five-day event will allow for all five sessions to be held. Then the SenseMaker lead will need to finalize the signification framework digitally so it is ready for collection. In some SenseMaker processes, a full day of training will be dedicated to working with facilitators to translate the signification framework accurately into the interview language. In the Central African Republic, the interview language was Sango, but

Table 23. Training content for the four competencies

	CONTENT	COMPETENCIES STRENGTHENED
Session 1	**INTRODUCTION** 1.1. Welcome 1.2. Introduce participants 1.3. Experience exchange 1.4. Introduction	Social and emotional
Session 2	**SENSEMAKER BASICS** 2.1. Understanding complexity 2.2. Why SenseMaker? 2.3. Key features of SenseMaker 2.4. Overview of the SenseMaker process	Change-related Technical
Session 3	**PURPOSE, LEARNING QUESTIONS & ANALYTICAL FRAMING** 3.1. Presentation of purpose of the SenseMaker project and learning questions 3.2. Analytical framing that underpins the project	Technical
Session 4	**UNDERSTANDING THE SIGNIFICATION FRAMEWORK** 4.1. Experiencing the signification framework 4.2. Signification framework on paper and digitally 4.3. Facilitating the process 4.4. Ethical considerations, safety, and data protection 4.5. Clarifying terminology and translation	Methodological Social and emotional Technical
Session 5	**PRACTICE AND USER TESTING** 5.1. Organizing the practice and final user test, including ethics and use of the devices 5.2. Practice and final user test 5.3. Feedback to facilitators on their practice and final troubleshooting 5.4. Feedback from facilitators for final signification framework review, including suggestions for more precise translation	Methodological Social and emotional Change-related Technical

the digital version of the signification framework was in French, as preferred by the facilitators who were fluent in both languages. Similarly, in Kenya, Uganda, Zambia, and Malawi, bilingual facilitators were found who could interview respondents in their own languages, while keeping the digital version of the signification framework in English. In many other experiences, the signification framework is fully designed in or translated to the collection language.

Recommendations for quality training

Investing in quality training is worthwhile. Experience has shown the following elements to be effective.
- Design and facilitate the workshop using interactive techniques and exercises that encourage participants to be active problem solvers. Create short, attractive presentations that keep participants engaged and promote an experiential process.
- Early on in the workshop, create an opportunity for the facilitators to experience the draft signification framework by answering the questions themselves and then sharing and self-signifying their narratives. This personal experience will help facilitators relate to respondents and give them ideas of how to facilitate the process.
- Together with the facilitators, draft a short introduction explaining the purpose of the SenseMaker process. Facilitators can use this to explain the process quickly and clearly to respondents.
- Use familiar examples to demonstrate and practice the different types of signifier questions.
- Prepare practical exercises to promote experiential learning.
- Use flipcharts and other materials to explain the signification framework and practice with it.
- Prepare a handout of the glossary of SenseMaker terms (see the glossary at the front of this guide) and include it in the facilitator manual.

Step 3: Facilitating the Collection Process

This section describes the collection scenarios: direct distribution, face-to-face facilitation, remote facilitation, and group settings.

Directly distributing the signification framework

Directly distributing the signification framework online works well in settings where respondents have easy access to technology, are literate, and are willing to share their experiences and stories. Direct distribution usually requires a respondent list with email addresses and a URL. The URL can be added to a webpage or a newsletter or shared in a blog or social media post.

Direct distribution requires a very clear set of instructions, especially on how to respond to signifier-type questions. Box 10 shows how this can be done for a triad using the example of tea-milk-sugar. These three response options can be adapted to what respondents will be familiar with.

Box 10. Explaining a triad question in online collection

For triad questions, place a mark inside the shape that best reflects the experience you described, balancing the relative importance of all three corners. The closer the mark is to a statement, the more relevance this statement has for your experience. To get you started, practice placing the mark to reflect your preferences in the first shape below, then move to the questions on the next page. If a question does not relate to the experience you shared, or none of the three options are relevant, mark the N/A box.

Please note we are only interested in the items listed for each question. For example, for this study we are only interested in the sleeping-working-preparing/consuming food combination, although a day can include other activities. Below is the example to get you started. Please reflect on the situation you shared and place a marker in the position that most relates to this situation. The closer the ball is to a corner, the stronger this element is. If all elements are equally important, place the marker in the middle. Click 'N/A' if a question does not apply to your situation.

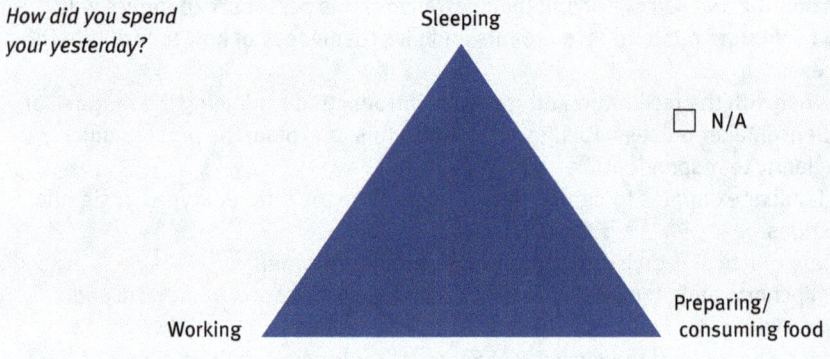

Direct distribution is easier to manage than facilitated collection. It can reach more respondents and people in other geographic areas, while requiring less preparation, fewer resources, and less time. However, it is also less likely to guarantee a high response rate and relies heavily on continuous monitoring and some form of collection management process (for example marketing or reminders).

Prompting people to respond is one of the most underestimated challenges of the direct distribution process. There is no one-size-fits-all recommendation on how to deal with this: some find regular reminders helpful, some share snapshots of preliminary results, and others create a reward process.

Face-to-face facilitation

A key feature of SenseMaker is the visualization tools: the sliders, the sliders with stones, the canvases with stones, and the triads. Especially with lower literacy respondents, but also with those with more literacy level, it can work well to draw these visuals on the ground, on whiteboards, or on flipcharts. Experience has shown that drawing or placing sliders, triads, and canvases on the ground can help respondents to better understand these types of signifier questions. This is a good optional practice, but may not be possible due to limited space, a dirty floor, or if people cannot bend over (elderly, people with a disability or breastfeeding mothers). This section describes how to explain the questions on the ground, with adaptations possible for needs and context.

Starting an interview

A good first impression is critical to establishing the rapport, trust, and confidence that enables respondents to feel comfortable sharing their experiences. Having a clear introduction to the SenseMaker process and its purpose is essential for giving facilitators the confidence they need to work with respondents.

Part of building trust involves obtaining the respondent's consent to participate. This is part of the introduction to the interview. It begins with a short explanation of the process and the instructions for it. Then, before asking any questions, the facilitator asks the respondent for their consent to participate. This explanation should also be provided in the introduction to the signification framework. A second consent request concerns the narrative, and whether it may be shared with others (see 'Consent to share the narrative' section below).

Participants must agree to take part in the study and give permission to the facilitators to have their data collected, stored, and used for publication. As part of this process, participants must be provided with sufficient information to make an informed decision. One option is to give them a Participant Information Sheet in advance, detailing what the study is about, how the data will be stored and used, how confidentiality and anonymity will be preserved, and emphasizing that participation is voluntary, and explaining how to withdraw at any time. Where literacy rates make this difficult, the information must be shared verbally.

Consent must be voluntary: no pressure or coercion may be applied. Consent is particularly important and more complex when researching vulnerable groups, such as children or minors, people with disabilities, mental illness, prisoners, ethnic minorities, or homeless people. It is essential to record consent. Written consent is preferred, but verbal consent (which should be witnessed and audio-recorded) may be obtained instead when, for example, the participants are illiterate. If photos are going to be taken during the process, and particularly if some will be used for publications, specific consent must be sought.

If a community leader, staff member, or official accompanies the facilitator in order to introduce them to the respondent, the facilitator will need to explain in a respectful way that the interview needs to take place without them. This helps to avoid community leaders exerting influence during an interview, and ensures respondent privacy and safety. However, avoid being alone in the interview space with the respondent. Being in sight of other people reduces the risk of compromising the safety of respondents or facilitators, although it may not be the ideal option for other reasons. Agreement on this should form part of the training.

When using SenseMaker for evaluations or assessments, it is particularly important to let respondents know that there are no right or wrong answers to any question. Being clear about how the information will be used, and for what purpose, can help reduce potential response bias. Respondents may overemphasize positive results if they believe an evaluation is taking place to determine whether a further phase of a project should take place, or if they think that doing so may benefit them or their community, or that not doing so will be to their or their community's detriment.

Prompting for the narrative

The narratives shared by respondents about their personal experiences form the basis of the entire self-signification process. Knowing how to clearly request a narrative, and encouraging respondents to share one, is thus a crucial step that will determine the quality of the interview. A good narrative describes a single, factual, personal experience of the respondent, rather than general opinions or accounts of multiple experiences. Table 24 describes the steps for drawing out the narrative with a prompter. The respondent must give explicit permission for audio recording, if used, as voice recognition may expose them to different risks than documentation.

Ask for the story title

Once the narrative has been finalized, ask for a title if it is in the signification framework. The following formulation has proven useful in prompting respondents in different places to provide titles for their narratives:

Now that you have shared your story, what three to five words come to mind that you would use to give your story a title?

The title must be provided by the respondents themselves, and not suggested or forced. The title can be revealing and can provide important insights into the experience that has been shared. In addition, it can be used for finding narratives in the dataset during the sensemaking process. Sometimes respondents are uneasy or may find it odd to give their experience a title. One approach that has worked well is to mention that songs have titles, and that the idea of giving a story a title is the same.

Consent to share the narrative

Getting respondents' consent to share their story anonymously with third parties is essential if the narratives are to be used for interpretation by stakeholders. This also means that the narratives can be included in any document or presentation or used for advocacy work. For this reason, facilitators must explain clearly to respondents that, even though their narrative will always remain anonymous, their story may be shared for analysis and interpretation, perhaps in different publications. The facilitator will ask for their consent using a multiple-choice question: no sharing, for analysis, in public. Once the respondent has shared their narrative about an experience that responds to the prompter, and has consented to continue with the interview, the types of signifier questions discussed in the Design chapter are used to collect additional layers of information about the experience. The

Table 24. Encouraging respondents to share a narrative

		TIPS AND RECOMMENDATIONS
Step 1	Ask the prompter	• Sit in order to create a safe setting. This may be side by side or at a respectful distance, in accordance with cultural norms. • Try to make regular eye contact to reassure respondents that you are listening to and interested in the experience that they are sharing. • Explain that this question requests a single, personal and lived experience. • Ask the prompter exactly as it is written in the signification framework, as it was carefully developed and tested during the Design phase. For consistency, it should be asked in the same way with all respondents. • After asking the prompter, give the respondent time to think deeply and carefully, and to decide what experience they want to share. This may take some time. • If necessary, repeat the question, but let the respondent think. Don't overwhelm them by asking it repeatedly. • Allow respondents to tell you what is important to them and avoid proposing to them what experiences they should share. • Depending on the prompter, the facilitator might help the respondent to prioritize a specific issue, such as a behavior change, a problem addressed by the community, a decision, or a shock or a stressor.
Step 2	Listen while taking notes	• Draft the narrative first on paper (optional), writing it up as it is told by the respondent. • Document the narrative with the wording used by the respondent.
Step 3	Read the narrative and revise it as necessary	• Organize the narrative, read it back from your notes, and ask the respondent if it has been captured accurately, or if it needs to be adjusted or expanded. • Make all the changes requested by the respondent. • If follow-up questions are included with the prompter, use them to probe for additional details. • Check with the respondent that this is the final version before moving on to the next question. • Ask the respondent for consent to share the story with others.
Step 4	Edit the narrative and save the signification framework	• Once you have finished with all questions, thank the respondent and leave. Find a quiet place, return to the prompter, and if you were unable to enter it, type in the narrative. If needed, listen to the audio recording you might have made again to complete the story with some details. • After you have documented the narrative, go to the end of the signification framework and save the participant's responses.

following sections explain in detail the protocols for facilitating each type of signifier question: slider, slider with stones, canvas with stones, and triad.

Facilitating a slider signifier question

When facilitating the first slider, helping respondents to visualize it is an effective way to explain the question. Draw a straight line on the ground with any available material and use cards or a symbol to label the two extremes. Use the labels for the first slider. The line should be long enough to allow the respondent to walk along it. Then place a marker in the middle of the line (Table 25) and follow these steps.

Step 1: Read the question exactly as written.

Step 2: There are two options.
- If the slider measures the degree of the same dimension, for example no influence at all versus very high influence, then ask the respondent to stand at one extreme and move towards the other end to the extent of influence or relevance. As an example, you can ask "how much coffee did you have this morning?" The answer can range from no coffee at all (an empty cup) or a full cup.
- If the slider relates to two dimensions (e.g. "the women sold their produce only at home or only at the market"), ask the respondent to stand at the midpoint of the slider and to move toward the element that represents the experience shared in the narrative. Explain that the closer they move to one element, the more relevant or applicable that element is to the experience in the narrative. Standing in the middle means that the elements are equally applicable. In terms of the cup of coffee, the two dimensions represent coffee and milk: one extreme represents a cup filled only with coffee, and the other extreme refers to a cup filled only with milk.

Step 3: Once the respondent has identified a point on the line, ask them to place a dot on the slider (if collecting on paper) or to move the slider on the device, so that it corresponds with the location indicated on the ground.

Facilitating a slider-with-stones signifier question

A slider with stones is a type of slider with multiple response options, or 'stones', that are placed along the slider. To facilitate these, additional cards need to be prepared for each of the options. These cards or stones can then be placed along the slider, following these steps:

Step 1: Read the question as written.

Step 2: Select cards or options as follows.
- If the question asks for the respondent to only place the options that apply to their own experience, ask them to select only those stones that apply.
- If the question asks the respondents to place all the stones on the slider, use all the stones.

Step 3: With the selected cards or options in hand, ask the respondent to stand at the midpoint of the slider and to select one card at a time, moving toward the element that represents the experience shared in the narrative. Explain that the closer they move to one end, the more relevant or applicable that element is to the experience in the narrative. Standing in the middle means that the elements are equally applicable for that option.

Step 4: Once the respondent has selected a position along the line, ask them to place a dot on the slider (if collecting on paper) or to move the slider on the device so that it corresponds with the location indicated on the ground.

Step 5: Repeat steps 2 to 4 for each option selected.

Table 25. Facilitating a slider signifier question

Facilitating a slider on the ground	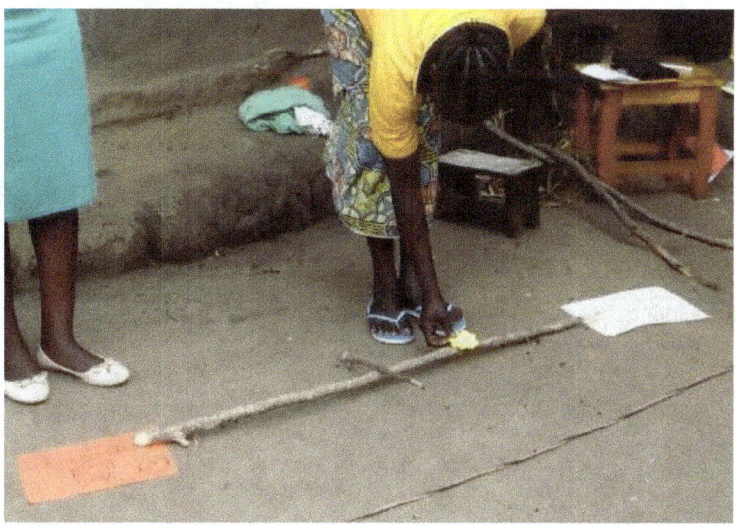
A slider as it appears on a tablet	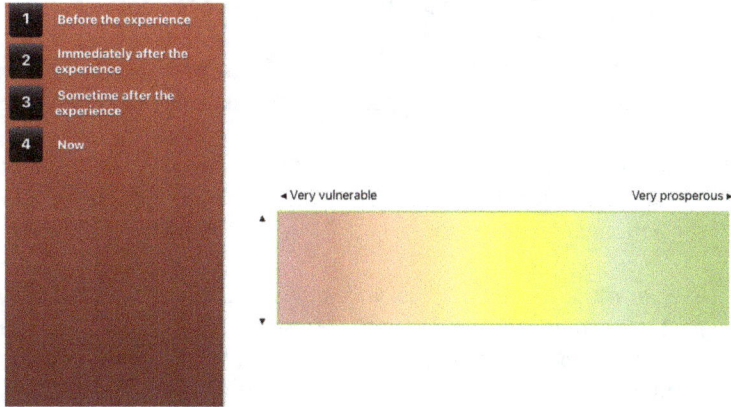

Figure 12. Screenshot of a canvas with stones

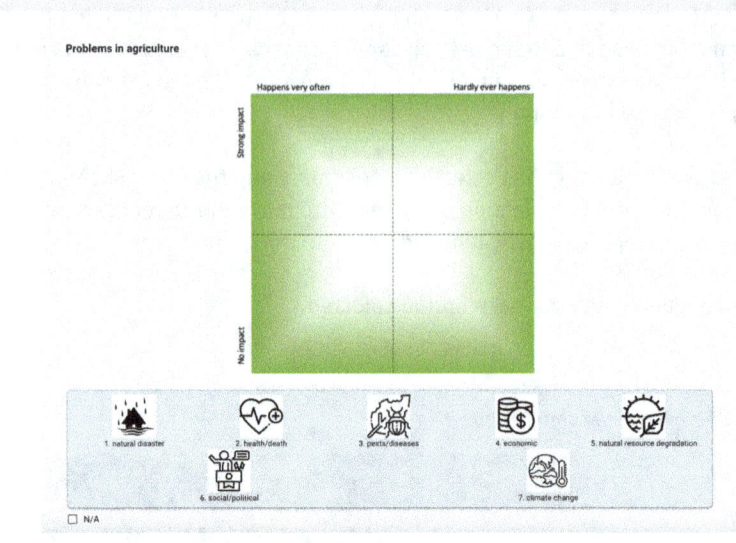

Facilitating a canvas-with-stones signifier question

This question takes some effort to understand, so facilitating it visually can help respondents make a considered response. Before facilitating the first question of this type, draw an axis on the ground with any available material and label the four ends of the lines using cards. Ensure that the lines are long enough to allow the respondent to walk along them (Table 26). Then follow these steps.

Step 1: Read the question as written.

Step 2: If the question has been designed so that the respondent must only work with the options relevant to them (and not all options), the respondent should select those that apply to their experience. If all options are to be considered, use all the stones.

Step 3: With one of the selected cards, post-its, or stones in hand, ask the respondent to stand at the midpoint of the X-axis (which is the horizontal axis) and move along that axis toward the element that is most relevant or applicable to their narrative. Explain that the closer they stand to the end, the stronger the degree to which that element is relevant or applicable to their experience (see movement 1 in the bottom diagram in Table 26).

Step 4: While still holding the same option, but using a second copy of the card, post-it, or stone, ask the respondent to stand at the midpoint on the Y-axis and to move along that axis toward the element that is most relevant or applicable to their narrative. Explain that the closer to the end they stand, the stronger the degree to which that element is relevant or applicable to their experience (see movement 2 in the bottom diagram in Table 26).

Step 5: Now draw a line parallel to the Y-axis that passes through the point marked on the X-axis; also draw a line parallel to the X-axis passing through the point marked on the Y-axis. Note the point at which these lines intersect (see point 3 in the bottom diagram in Table 26).

Step 6: Ask the respondent to transfer this point to the device or the paper. The location on the device or paper should correspond to the location marked on the ground. Figure 12 shows an example of how a canvas with stones looks online. Ask the respondent what the location of the dot means, supporting them to confirm whether the location represents what they want to say.

Step 7: Repeat steps 2 through 6 for each option selected, or for all options, depending on how the question was designed.

Table 26. Facilitating a canvas-with-stones signifier question

Facilitating a canvas with stones on the ground	
Step-by-step facilitation of a canvas with stones	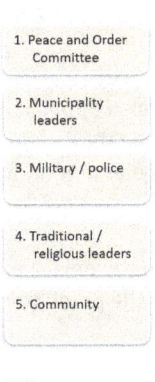 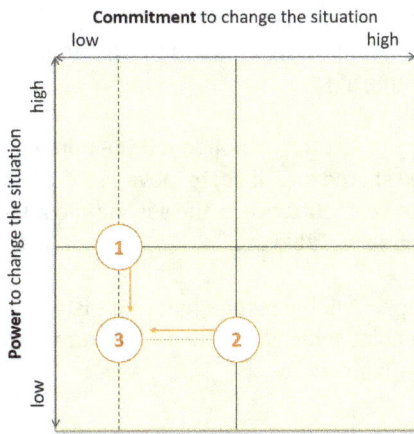

A Practical Guide for Using SenseMaker 115

Facilitating a triad signifier question

A signification framework will typically have a few triad questions. Their facilitation can be a little tricky. Explaining the first triad in some detail will make it easier for the respondent to understand and respond to subsequent triad questions.

One effective way to facilitate the first triad is to recreate it on the ground, using any available material—such as rope, sticks, or sugarcane—to create an equilateral triangle, and then using cards or pictures to label the three corners. Ensure that each side of the triad is similar in length and that the lines are straight. This helps guide the respondent to where their response best fits (Table 27). The aim is to draw out a more accurate response by allowing the person to reflect and sense their response visually and physically. It is not necessary to be mathematically precise, but rather about representing a tendency. The triad should be large enough to ensure sufficient space between the three corners. The response can be facilitated by the following steps. Once the respondent understands the triad well and feels comfortable with the digital device, then this can take place directly with the on-screen triad.

Step 1: Read the question as written.

Step 2: Ask the respondent if any of the three elements identified on the corners of the triad applies to the experience they shared in the narrative. If none of them apply, select the 'not applicable' option. If at least one of them applies, continue to the next step.

Step 3: Ask the respondent to select the element that initially feels like it is most relevant or applicable to the narrative they have shared, and to stand in that corner (movement 1 in the middle diagram in Table 27).

Step 4: Ask the respondent to select the second most important element in the experience shared, and to move along the side of the triangle toward the second element. Explain that the nearer they are to that second element, the more relevant or applicable it is in relation to the element in the first corner. A mark can be placed at the respondent's location. If it is in the middle, confirm that this means that the two elements are equally relevant or applicable (movement 2 in the middle diagram in Table 27).

Step 5: Ask the respondent if the third element is also applicable to the experience they shared and, if so, to move in the direction of the third element, according to its relative importance to the second-most important element (movement 3 in the first diagram in Table 27).

Step 6: Ask the respondent to transfer the point to the device or paper. Ensure that the point selected on the device corresponds with the point arrived at on the ground (see Table 27).

Table 27. Facilitating a triad signifier question

Facilitating a canvas with stones on the ground	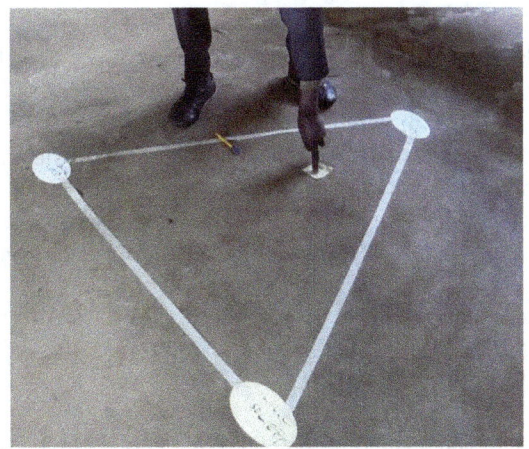
Step-by-step facilitation of a triad	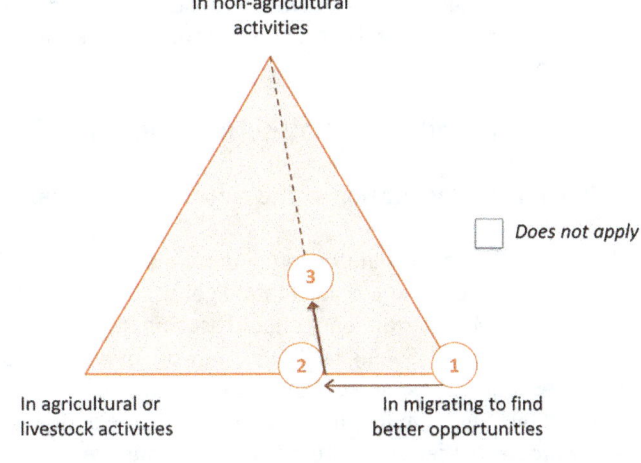
Screenshot of a triad as it appears on a tablet	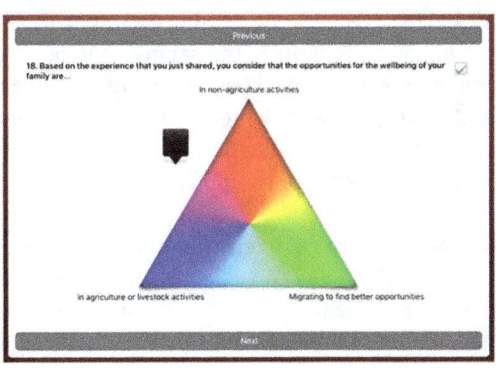

Remote facilitation

Remote facilitation is an alternative when face-to-face facilitation is not possible. The facilitation follows the same protocol described above for a face-to-face facilitation, but it is conducted using a chat-based application such as Skype, Teams or Zoom. The facilitator in this case opens Collector using the URL for the designed signification framework and shares their screen with the respondent. This requires the respondent to have internet access, and a computer or tablet with the selected chat-based application. This process allows respondents to listen the facilitator, orally share their narrative, and see the questions in the facilitator's screen while they follow the protocol to facilitate each signifier question, and to provide their answers.

Facilitation in group settings

If respondents are experienced and literate enough to manage devices or paper versions on their own, they can be guided in a group setting through the collection process. The main facilitator explains this with a whiteboard, a flipchart, or by projecting the collection app question by question. Collection of data in a group setting can also be organized and facilitated through online sessions (e.g. through applications such as Zoom). The protocols for facilitating prompters, triads, sliders, sliders with stones, and canvas with stones are the same in the case of face-to-face facilitation.

Step 4: Monitoring Collection and Ensuring Data Quality

Supervising facilitation of the collection process

During collection, facilitators often require support and initial guidance. During the first days of collection, as facilitators get used to the collection process, someone with SenseMaker experience should accompany them to provide support and initial trouble-shooting. Seeing facilitators at work provides invaluable insights into how they encourage responses, how they take care to explain signifier questions, and how they build rapport with respondents. At the end of each day, the team discusses any problems they encountered, and solutions are shared and agreed upon. Challenges can include last-minute uncertainty about how to introduce a particular question, the speed of facilitation, dealing with specific dynamics between individuals, finding respondents in the sample, and technical support on the use of devices and troubleshooting issues in their functioning and/or uploading of the collected data. Time spent with the team during these initial days is time very well spent, as it will ensure data quality throughout. For the remainder of the collection process, a collection supervisor should coordinate and support the process.

Monitoring collection is critical to ensuring the quality of the narratives, the completeness of the data, and consistency. There are two ways to do this: by supervising and observing facilitators in action and by looking at the data on a daily basis.

Assuring data and collection quality

Ensuring the completeness and quality of the data is an important task during collection that can be undertaken remotely. It is strongly recommended that a person on the team is specifically tasked with this.

Assuring data quality

Data quality assurance involves looking at the dataset early on. Aspects to check on include:

- **Data.** Are the data uploading correctly? For example, do all variables have the right labels visible in the dataset? Are the expected number of observations present, or are some missing? Are there any blank or half-completed entries that need to be investigated? Compare the number of collected datasets to the number uploaded for each facilitator and device.
- **Technical problems.** Are there any technical problems reported by facilitators that can be identified in the dataset? For example, perhaps it is not clear if an entry was saved, or perhaps a response option did not correctly display on a collection device.
- **Narrative quality.** Are the narratives of good quality? They should be relevant, have enough length and detail, and not be repetitive.

It can also be helpful to look at the patterns that emerge early on by checking the visualizations for core SenseMaker questions and the use of MCQs. Some points to consider are listed below.

- Are most triad question responses concentrated in the middle of the triangle, or in a specific corner? See Figure 13 for a comparison of concentrated responses with spread responses. Concentrated responses may mean that the facilitator is not following the collection protocols for core SenseMaker questions. It may also mean that the question does not work in that specific setting or with that group of respondents.
- In slider, slider-with-stones, and canvas questions, are there too many responses at one or both extremes or in the center?
- Are there too many 'Not Applicable' responses, especially for signifier questions for which this was not expected?
- In slider-with-stones and canvas-with-stones questions, are all the stones being used when all are required?
- In slider-with-stones and canvas-with-stones questions, are more stones being used than allowed?
- Is the 'Other' option used too often? This may indicate that the facilitators are not clear about the meaning of the options, or that the MCQ design missed crucial topics.

Figure 13. Concentrated and spread response patterns

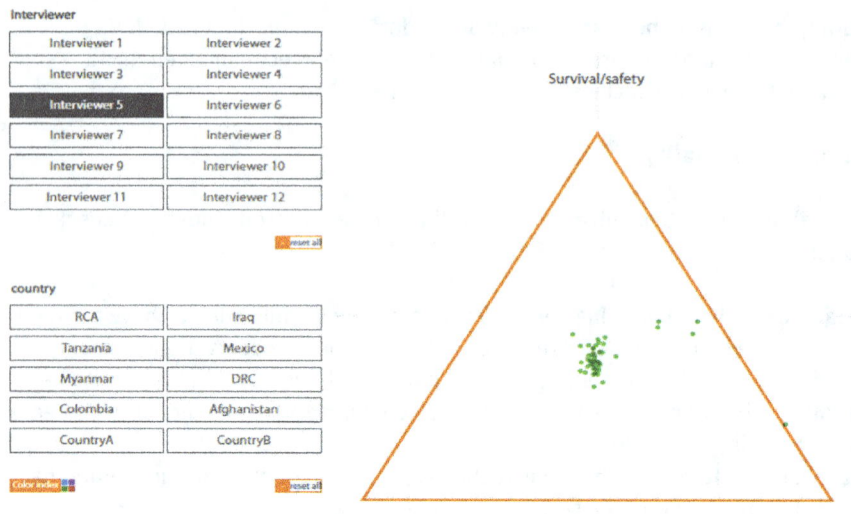

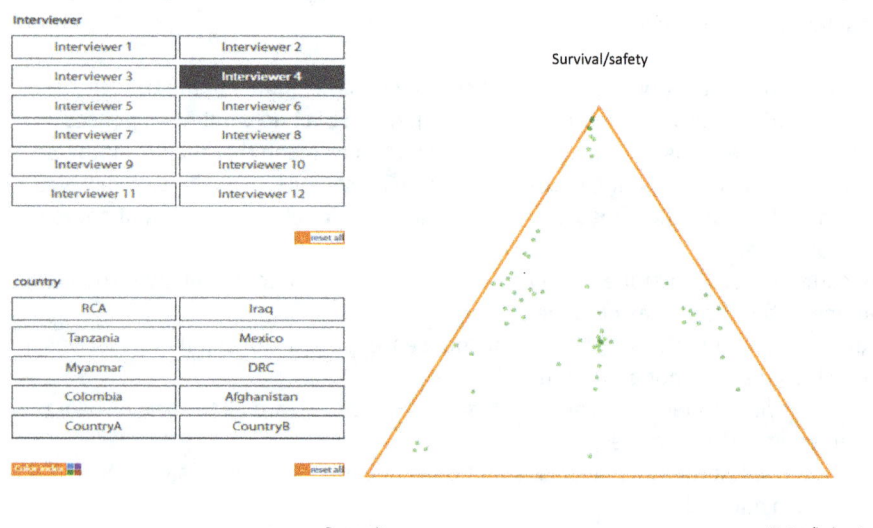

120   The Learning Power of Listening

Monitoring the collection process

It is important to track if collection is advancing as planned, or whether delays require the plan to be adjusted. Delays may be related to a range of issues—for example, there may be unexpected difficulties related to access to facilitators, longer interview times, a failure to achieve anticipated groups counts, poor internet connection to upload the datasets for quality check, or difficulties accessing communities due to road conditions or security issues.

Also ensure the sampling strategy is being fulfilled. This can be taken care of during the design phase by adding a question on key groups, if these are not covered by the sociodemographic questions.

Phase 3: Collection

Phase 4: Sensemaking

- 124 **Sensemaking Principles**
- 125 **Deciding on the Sensemaking Strategy**
- 129 **Preparing for Sensemaking**
- 131 **Building Block 1: Primary Analysis**
- 158 **Building Block 2: Collective Interpretation**
- 168 **Building Block 3: Comprehensive Analysis**
- 178 **Building Block 4: Communication and Use**

Sensemaking is the collective process of giving meaning to data to inform decisions and actions, an exciting phase when patterns form, ideas are validated, and surprises emerge.

Phase 4: Sensemaking

Once all the data are collected, cleaned, and downloaded, the process of making sense of the narratives and the responses to the signifier questions can begin. Sensemaking is the collective process of giving meaning to data and emerging knowledge in order to make decisions and act on the findings. This is an exciting phase when patterns form, ideas are validated, and surprises emerge. The analysis of the narratives and the data generated by the self-signification process can be as detailed and layered as time, resources, and capacities allow.

The sensemaking process has four building blocks: primary analysis, collective interpretation, comprehensive analysis, and communication and use (Figure 14). This chapter discusses each of these building blocks in detail, providing guidance on how to carry them out. First, it discusses the sensemaking principles, the elements of a sensemaking strategy, and the considerations for its design, as well as the logistics required to prepare and facilitate the Sensemaking phase.

The time and financial resources invested in the preparation, design and collection will only be worthwhile if the data are analyzed properly and interpreted from different perspectives, and if insights are communicated and used effectively. Clarifying who best to involve in what aspects of sensemaking – with support for those to whom this is new – will ensure that the sensemaking benefits optimally from different stakeholders' perspectives. Insights emerging during primary analysis and collective interpretation will offer ideas for more comprehensive analysis. With a sensemaking plan, the learning questions that shaped the SenseMaker process are more likely to be answered.

Figure 14. Components of the sensemaking phase

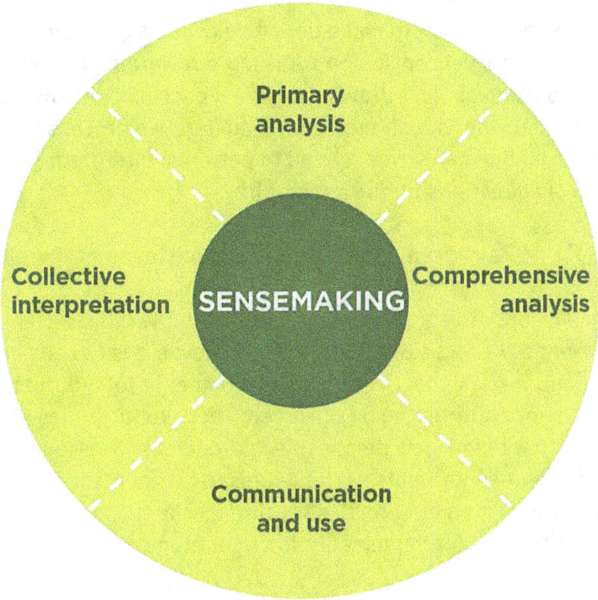

Sensemaking Principles

The sensemaking phase is a collective journey of asking, visualizing, examining, and recombining the qualitative and quantitative data that SenseMaker generates. The individual and collective reflections this process triggers should lead to new insights that inform decisions for programming, advocacy, or local action, as well as generating evidence for change. There are four important sensemaking principles that help ensure high-quality analysis, interpretation, and use.

Principle 1: Balance the approach to data analysis.

Sensemaking can take an exploratory route or a structured route to data analysis. Finding the right balance between the two has many benefits.

An exploratory approach allows: (1) interesting patterns to be identified, (2) new insights to be generated, (3) surprises and unexpected results to be found, (4) weak signals to be captured, (5) further avenues of inquiry to be generated, and (6) emergent concepts and frameworks to be identified.

A structured approach is shaped by the SenseMaker process objectives, learning questions, and the analytical framing that was designed, adjusted, or selected for the process. It intentionally uses questions, concepts, and relations between the concepts to filter the findings and test relationships between responses.

Any primary or comprehensive analysis needs a good balance between these two approaches. Primary analysis usually emphasizes the open-ended exploratory approach, while comprehensive analysis tends to use a more structured approach.

Principle 2: Delay definitive conclusions.

It can be very tempting to make definitive conclusions quickly, thus this can lead to incorrect and partial conclusions. It is more rewarding to hold back and allow data to reveal patterns before drawing any final conclusions. Any observation or finding needs to be further questioned during an iterative process that involves detecting patterns, reading narratives related to patterns, interpreting the findings, and raising new questions for further inquiry.

Principle 3: Pay attention to dominant patterns and weak signals.

It is usually easy to spot dominant patterns in the data. Insights based on these can then become the focus of conclusions. However, it is equally important to note and understand weak signals, where small clusters or total outliers that diverge from the dominant patterns can be observed. These outliers may give clues to emergent practices that teams may decide to explore further for scaling or amplification, or they may represent threats or challenges to be dampened if they are to be prevented from growing. Emergent practices or threats can thus form the basis of new ideas and opportunities for implementation or strategy.

Principle 4: Find the best option under the circumstances for involving stakeholders in sensemaking.

Involving key stakeholders is essential to generating new insights, bringing additional depth to the analysis, and properly interpreting the findings. New stakeholders can stimulate discussion, help capture reflections from different perspectives, and provide useful feedback for further inquiry. Moreover, joint interpretation can create a sense of ownership, which can support the uptake of findings for making decisions and taking action. This principle is discussed in more detail in the Collective interpretation section below.

Deciding on the Sensemaking Strategy

Planning for sensemaking helps ensure quality in the analysis and interpretation of the findings. It also contributes to successful communication and use of the findings in line with the purpose of the SenseMaker process purpose. During the Preparation phase, general decisions were made about the Sensemaking phase. However, it is now important to revisit these decisions and agree on a more detailed sensemaking strategy. The design of the strategy will be informed by:
- the purpose of the SenseMaker process,
- the learning questions that guide the study,
- the stakeholders, and how they anticipate using the findings,
- the expertise of the core team and the technical support available from skilled SenseMaker practitioners, and
- the resources and time available.

This strategy needs to clearly state:
- how analysis will be approached in the sensemaking phase,
- the degree and nature of stakeholder participation,
- the balance between analyzing quantitative and qualitative data, and
- the visualization and analytical software required.

Analysis approach

How exploratory or structured will the analysis be?

Purely exploratory ———————————————————— Purely structured

The analysis approach to sensemaking can be more exploratory or more structured, but it is recommended that a combination of the two is used (see Principle 1). In practice, sensemaking involves moving back and forth between being open to whatever the data shows—the exploratory approach—and focusing on specific questions or a particular analysis logic—the structured approach. This balance helps ensure unexpected findings are not missed, while generating insights that address more specific SenseMaker process objectives and learning questions. When using a structured approach, it is good practice to develop an analysis pathway that can be informed by the analytical framing. This will reduce the risk of following a potentially unlimited number of leads.

Degree and nature of stakeholder participation

Who will be involved in sensemaking?

Only the core team — All stakeholders

Some sensemaking activities can be conducted by an individual member of the core team, while others require the entire core team, thematic experts, or wider participation from the different stakeholders. The more interactive the analysis, the clearer the sensemaking strategy needs to be, regarding who to involve, when to involve them, for what purpose, and how best to prepare for their involvement. Having key stakeholders play a part in interpreting findings is good practice that greatly improves the quality of sensemaking and promotes the use of the findings.

Combination of quantitative and qualitative data

How much emphasis will be given to quantitative vis-à-vis qualitative data analysis?

Only quantitative analysis — Only qualitative analysis

Sensemaking normally begins with pattern detection in signifier responses, combined with an initial scan of the narratives. This is followed by qualitative analysis of sets of stories from selected areas of the patterns, looking for dominant responses or outliers, or using signifier MCQs; or quantitative analysis on the basis of MCQs and signifier data. The analysis team must decide how the pattern and narrative analyses will be sequenced and used in the sensemaking process, as well as the balance between looking at quantitative data (patterns and MCQs) and qualitative data (narratives).

Analytical and visualization software

What software will be used?

Only SenseMaker software — Mix of specialized reporting analysis and software

The analytical and visualization software to be used in analysis should be suitable for the sensemaking approach and for the selected combination of qualitative and quantitative analysis. Software options include The Cynefin Company proprietary tools for data visualization as well as third-party visualization tools (such as Tableau and PowerBI), quantitative analysis tools (e.g. R and SPSS/Stata), and qualitative text analysis tools (like NVivo and Atlas.ti). More information on some of these software options is provided in Table 28. It is important to make decisions on software well in advance, in order to ensure that the necessary software is available and installed at the beginning of this phase. Note that software is continually changing for all these tools. For example, as the Guide went to press, the analytical software had just shifted to a Dashboard for quick browsing of patterns and a Workbench for analytical depth.

Table 28. Software options for visualization and analysis

SOFTWARE CAPABILITIES	Access requirements	Internet connectivity	Dataset type
Dashboard and Workbench (SenseMaker Suite) • Interactive visualization of all core SenseMaker questions and corresponding narratives • Count of responses per questions • Filtering and disaggregation by any MCQ • X–Y plot that show trends, correlations or associations, dominant patterns, and weak signals • Two-dimensional density plots (scatter plots, distribution plots, contour maps, heat maps).	Individual SenseMaker account set up by The Cynefin Company	Online application	Data embedded in application
COST Included in SM license	**EASE OF USE** Easy with basic training		
Excel • MCQ plot generation • Customized MCQ cross-tabulation • Basic statistical functions • Generation of new variables	Dataset	Offline application	Dataset
COST Included in MS Office package	**EASE OF USE**		
PowerBI • Interactive visualization of all core SenseMaker questions and corresponding narratives • Count of responses per questions • MCQ cross-tabulation • Filtering and disaggregation by any MCQ	Dataset	Offline application	Dataset
COST Included in MS Office corporate packages	**EASE OF USE** Medium difficulty. Training and practice needed to design dashboards; easy to access and view		

continued ⇢

	SOFTWARE CAPABILITIES	Access requirements	Internet connectivity	Dataset type
Tableau	• Customized visualization of signifier questions and corresponding narratives • MCQ cross-tabulation • Filtering with MCQs • Customized graphs • Interactive visualization	Dataset	Offline application	Dataset
	COST Free to view and interact with, but license required for setup	**EASE OF USE** Difficult; training and practice are needed to design the dashboards; easy to access and view		
R	• Visualization of all core SenseMaker questions and corresponding narratives • Count of responses per questions • MCQ cross-tabulation • Filtering and disaggregation by any MCQ • Two-dimensional density plots (scatter plots, distribution plots, contour maps*, heat maps). • Generation of new variables • Basic and advanced statistical analysis	Dataset	Offline application	Dataset
	COST Open source/ Free	**EASE OF USE** Difficult; training and practice needed		
SPSS/Stata	• Customized visualization of core SenseMaker questions • Two-dimensional plots • Generation of new variables • Basic and advanced statistical analysis	Dataset	Offline application	Dataset
	COST License required	**EASE OF USE** Difficult; training and practice needed; requires statistical knowledge		

Contour maps are two-dimensional density plots that show the areas of concentration of different responses, visualizing dominant and strong patterns and differentiating them from weak signals.

Preparing for Sensemaking

Once the core team decides on the sensemaking strategy and revises and finalizes the plan for this phase of the SenseMaker process, some key preparation needs to be made. This includes: (1) preparing the data for analysis, and (2) ensuring the selected software has been procured and is ready for use.

Preparing the data for analysis

The collected narratives and answers from the self-signification process are stored online. Datasets can be downloaded as comma separated value (.csv) files.

Before beginning analysis, the data are prepared. This may include the following actions:
- cleaning the dataset;
- adding translated, transcribed, and edited narratives;
- creating new variables based on the collected data and adding them to the master file;
- merging datasets;
- downloading datasets;
- importing datasets.

Each of these actions is described below with an explanation of what it involves and key recommendations.

Data cleaning

It is recommended that changes or additions to the collected dataset are made to the Master dataset. These changes are irreversible. Teams may choose to keep a record of any changes that were made, as well as local copies of older versions securely on a local drive.

Data cleaning may involve:
- Reconciling the number of observations in the dataset with the collection records.
- Identifying and deleting duplicate entries, as some facilitators may have mistakenly uploaded an entry more than once. This can happen when an internet connection is poor.
- Identifying and deleting empty and test entries.
- Reviewing and reclassifying free text ('other') responses to multiple-choice questions.

Adding translated, transcribed, and edited narratives

Narratives collected in a language different to that used in the Sensemaking phase will need to be transcribed, translated, and incorporated into a dataset. In the proprietary software, these need to be added to the master file.

Creating new variables based on the collected data and adding them to the master file

Sometimes, a new variable must be added to the dataset. For example, in a set of studies on resilience, respondents were asked how they felt before facing a shock or stressor, immediately after, sometime after, and at present. Primary analysis showed that, based on these responses, participants followed different trajectories in their advancement along a 'pathway to prosperity': prosperous (steadily improving), resilient (had a fall and rebounded, or rebounded better), or vulnerable (had a fall and rebounded worse, or collapsed). These trajectories became a new classification variable, with three options on how respondents coped over time. These three new categories were created and added to the dataset as an additional variable, allowing for analysis of new subsets of respondents. When a third party software is used for analysis and visualization, the dataset needs to be downloaded. However, new variables should not be introduced when these are external interpretations of narratives, as this would go against the principle of self-interpretation.

Merging the SenseMaker dataset with other datasets

In some cases, SenseMaker may also be used in combination with other methods, such as monitoring data, surveys, and secondary data. The SenseMaker-collected dataset must then be merged with those collected through other methods. If this is known in advance, it is best that a unique ID be added to the signification framework; this is then entered during the Collection phase. In this way, different datasets can be merged during the Sensemaking phase—using third-party software like Excel, R, or SPSS/Stata.

Exporting and importing the dataset

The dataset is ready for analysis once: (1) it has been cleaned; (2) the translated, transcribed, and edited narratives have been incorporated; and (3) the new variables created or merged from other datasets have been added to the master file. With the Dashboard and Workbench, data does not need to be downloaded and can be visualized and analyzed directly online. However, if analysis is to be conducted with non-SenseMaker proprietary software, the datasets can be exported as CSV files.

Ensuring that the selected software is procured and installed

As part of the sensemaking strategy, the core team needs to ensure that the analytical and visualization software selected for the chosen sensemaking strategy is available, procured, installed, and running. This will make the best use of the time allotted for the Sensemaking phase, specifically in the primary analysis, the collective interpretation, and the comprehensive analysis building blocks.

In addition to setting up the software, ensure that the sensemaking team has the following material ready for use:
- a copy of the signification framework, and
- the final dataset, cleaned and ready for analysis.

Building Block 1: Primary Analysis

Primary analysis usually takes an exploratory approach and is aimed at providing a bird's eye view of findings, enabling practitioners to describe and understand the main characteristics of the data. This involves characterizing respondents to better understand who they are. However, its main focus is presenting responses visually in the form of plots and graphs and in this way identifying dominant patterns and outliers, while also identifying where it is necessary to disaggregate responses and determining the variables that will be used to do this. This is undertaken by: (1) using visualization tools (plots and graphs), (2) using quantitative techniques (summary statistics with some basic level of disaggregation and correlations among selected variables), and (3) reading and analyzing sets of narratives from different groups of respondents, along with any text that has been entered in the 'other' field of the MCQs. The sets of narratives for analysis can be extracted by filtering them using MCQs or can be drawn by selecting responses from dominant clusters or from outliers.

Primary analysis has six aims.
1. To develop a basic understanding of respondents' sociodemographic characteristics by looking at the number and proportion of responses to sociodemographic questions (e.g. age, education levels, participation in a program).
2. To explore patterns of responses by visualizing and describing responses for each follow-up question: (a) multiple questions about the experience shared in the narrative (e.g. whether the respondent considers the experience to be positive, negative or neutral; the actions and decisions taken in the experience; and who made these decisions, and how); and (b) signifier questions (sliders, sliders with stones, canvases with stones, and triads) to generate a reflection process on the experience shared.
3. To explore patterns of responses for a subgroup of respondents of interest (e.g. only female respondents, or respondents who are younger than 30); or to compare subgroups of respondents (such as men versus women, or project participants versus nonparticipants).
4. To read and conduct textual analysis of groups of narratives (e.g. analyzing and comparing those narratives signified as 'positive' with those signified as 'negative') for the overall sample, or for a subset of the sample data.
5. To explore relationships between variables to visualize how likely people are to respond in one way to one question and in a different way to another question (e.g. how likely are people who considered that, in the experience shared, prioritized crops enabled them to increase sales to also consider that these crops enabled them to obtain better prices?).
6. To frame questions and identify issues that need to be further explored during collective interpretation or comprehensive analysis.

A good practice for primary analysis is to explore responses to all signifier questions. This simple first step provides a bird's eye view and may often lead to some unexpected findings. During this process, it can be helpful to start by letting each member of the sensemaking core team explore the data individually and to describe their observations, as this helps to reduce conformity within a team. The team can then share, discuss, and compare their observations, enriching each other's insights. Primary analysis requires at least one person with expertise in data analysis who understands the structure of the SenseMaker dataset and is skilled in using both SenseMaker-specific and other analytical software. This person can coordinate and support the primary analysis, while developing the capacity of the other team members. Primary analysis is an excellent opportunity for team members to familiarize themselves with the analytical process and to build their capacity.

Findings from primary analysis need to be documented for sharing with the SenseMaker process stakeholders, as described in the sensemaking strategy (see earlier in this chapter). These can be documented as short briefing papers, temporary reports, or annotated PowerPoint presentations, as described in the stakeholder analysis conducted during the Preparation phase. This will help to decide which insights are of interest for which stakeholder and how best to communicate them.

If the findings of the primary analysis are to be presented and discussed through collective interpretation, the core sensemaking team members should ensure these are clearly presented by incorporating the required information in each visual. This will include the question that generated the responses, clear labels for each visual, the sample size, the number of responses in each subset of responses (if disaggregated), and the percentages that each represents. In addition, teams may wish to include a short paragraph describing what the graph objectively portrays, in order to ensure that it is properly interpreted. There is extensive literature on data visualization that can be consulted to generate well-thought-out and properly presented visuals.

Steps for conducting primary analysis

A step-by-step process for conducting primary analysis is provided here. It is not meant to be restrictive, but to provide guidance, especially for new SenseMaker practitioners. Analysis processes are iterative and dynamic by nature, as preliminary findings give direction to and inform the subsequent steps, following the probe–sense–adjust approach to dealing with complexity.

Step 1: Visualize and describe the sociodemographic characteristics of respondents
Recommended software: Dashboard and Workbench, Excel, PowerBI/Tableau, R/SPSS/Stata

Visualizing and describing the socioeconomic characteristics of the respondents is important for two reasons. It can help determine whether the proportion of each subgroup of interest aligns with the sampling strategy. This is particularly important for studies that seek a certain degree or type of representation. It also helps identify dominant and underrepresented subsets of the sample data, which can be important for making valid generalizations. Describing the socioeconomic characteristics of respondents can also offer information on the respondents' characteristics, which can prove useful for two reasons.

They can help disaggregate findings so as to assess the differences between subsets of respondents. For example, in one study in Malawi it was observed that, although the majority of program participants were women and had received the same training as men, significant knowledge and skills gaps could be observed between the two groups. Thus, at the median, women had lower natural resource management, innovation, and marketing competencies than men, but had higher financial competencies.

They can help to contextualize and interpret the findings. For example, in a multi-country study in Malawi, Zambia, and Guatemala, it was found that a lack of skill in record keeping and analysis of farming results—such as the assessment of production, sales, costs, and net profit—was a major widespread competency gap. Connecting this finding with the results of an MCQ on the respondents' levels of formal education showed that most project participants were illiterate or could only read and write, and that the rest had only finished primary school, and thus helped explain these findings. With this better understanding of how project participants lacked this competency, the project team devised the innovative idea of supporting project participants to close this gap by including farming activities and costing and profit analysis in the financial education curricula.

Step 2: **Visualize and describe responses to multiple-choice signifier questions**
Recommended software: Dashboard and Workbench, Excel, PowerBI/Tableau, R/ SPSS/Stata

This step involves understanding the responses to MCQs on the narratives. These multiple-choice signifier questions are useful for two reasons. First, they can help to foster an understanding of the general nature of the narratives, as perceived by the respondents. Second, they provide additional layers of information about the experiences shared by respondents in their narratives. Some examples of MCQs used for this purpose follow:

Feelings and emotions. In a baseline study of a peacebuilding project on Mindanao Island in the Philippines, respondents were asked to indicate the feelings they associated with their experience about a conflict situation in their community (worried, hopeful, happy, sad, proud, frustrated, angry, or indifferent). The responses showed that half of the respondents were worried about the situation described in their stories, but also that a surprisingly high number of stories (30 percent) made people feel happy and hopeful. This generated insights about the type of conflicts and the way in which people dealt with them, which they perceived as positive. In addition, this MCQ about the associated feelings provided possibilities for the next SenseMaker collection cycles to track progression toward more positive-oriented stories (or not) in relation to project interventions.

Issues of importance for respondents. In an evaluation study of an initiative promoting gender-equitable social norms in Bangladesh, adolescent girls and boys were asked to share a recent challenging experience faced by a girl in the village (who could be either the respondent or another girl in the community). As a follow-up to the narrative, respondents were asked to tag the themes associated with their narratives (education, marriage, family relations, safety/security, income, romantic relationships, the girl's honor, freedom of movement, violence, friendship, or dowry).

This type of MCQ enabled a better understanding of the issues that were more important for boys and girls, and the differences between them. While 60 percent of the stories told by girls showed that education was a key issue for them, almost 60 percent of the stories shared by boys showed that marriage/relationship issues were more important for them. Further analysis showed that school and education were significantly connected to, and impacted on, what mattered in girls' lives (honor, relationships, future, dreams, income, and family relations).

Supporters or influencers. In a final evaluation of a project to support refugees who had arrived in Ecuador, respondents were asked about the relationships — whether with family or relatives, neighbors or friends, religious groups, community organizations, government organizations, the NGO implementing the project, or other NGOs — that were important in helping them recover from the challenging event shared in their experience. Most respondents mentioned the local NGO that implemented this initiative, followed in importance by family members or relatives, neighbors or friends, and then other NGOs. This led to the conclusion that, although not all the observed changes could be attributed to the initiative, it certainly made an important contribution to achieving them.

Type of events. In a multi-country study aimed at understanding and assessing resilience, an MCQ was used to identify the types of shock and stressor — drought, unpredictable rainfall, crop pests and disease, livestock disease, economic crisis, illness and death, flooding, and social conflict — present in the experiences shared in the narratives, which had the greatest effect on people's lives or livelihoods. The pattern of responses revealed important information about the dominance of climate-related shocks and stressors, which informed the program's design and implementation.

Time of events. A resilience study conducted in the Democratic Republic of the Congo to refine and implement a multi-year assistance program to reduce malnutrition made use of an MCQ to identify the types of shocks and stressors. This was followed by another MCQ to identify when these happened. The findings showed that the most important shocks that project participants faced were armed conflict, death, illness, and loss of financial or physical assets, that they had faced these shocks mainly one or two years previously, and that the shocks had continued to affect them in the previous year. This provided important information on the context in which this initiative was being implemented and the challenges it would need to overcome if it were to achieve its goals and objectives.

Second, these types of signifier question can also be useful in finding subsets of the dataset that may be of interest for exploring further or comparing to each other. For example, they can be used to cluster sets of narratives in order to conduct further textual analysis, or as filters to visualize and describe the patterns seen in other signifier questions. For example, signifier MCQs have been used to cluster and analyze narratives by both type of experience and type of shock or stressor.

Type of experience. In a multi-country study assessing the behavioral changes resulting from training, mentoring, and coaching activities, and their impact on people's livelihoods, respondents were asked if the experiences they shared were positive, negative, or neutral. This allowed a textual analysis to be conducted on the three corresponding sets of narratives, extracting the aspects that made them positive, negative, or neutral experiences in terms of context and individual competencies; the behaviors, decisions, and actions taken; and the outcomes achieved. These findings could then be compared.

Type of shock or stressor. In the multi-country study on resilience mentioned above, the shocks and stressors in the narratives that had the greatest impact on people's lives or livelihoods were used to cluster the responses by type of shock and stressor. These included: (1) stories about slow-onset stressors (drought, unpredictable or erratic rainfall, crop pests and disease, natural resource degradation, and social or ethnic conflict); (2) stories about rapid-onset shocks (strong winds, floods, cyclones, or hailstorms); and (3) stories about individual crises (economic crisis, illness, accidents, and death). These were then cross-referenced with coping actions, adaptive responses, or transformative strategies taken by respondents, in order to better understand if the type of shock or stressor affected respondents' actions, responses and strategies, as well as the resilience outcomes.

Step 3: Visualize and describe the responses to core SenseMaker questions
Recommended software: Dashboard and Workbench, PowerBI/Tableau, R

The process of generating and describing the patterns of responses to core SenseMaker questions (triad, slider, slider with stones, or canvas with stones) lies at the core of the primary analysis. SenseMaker collects quantitative and qualitative data from respondents who have shared narratives and responded to different types of signifier questions. As with conventional survey methods, these responses produce both categorical data (MCQs) and continuous data (triad, slider, slider with stones, or canvas with stones). These quantifiable data points are created by respondents tagging their own experiences. As with most research, the degree of confidence with which it is possible to make inferences from the data depends on the sampling strategy used and the size of the sample; these determine the level of confidence in the data and the error margin.

In SenseMaker terminology, 'patterns' refer to how each response is visualized in the shape of each type of signifier question (triad, slider, or canvas), based on its position, generating tight clusters that represent dominant responses or dispersed clusters that represent outliers or weak signals. Patterns do not necessarily need a certain number of data points to provide useful insights; this is especially true for subsets of respondents for which there are fewer data points, but that are important for responding to learning questions or testing assumptions.

Visualizations of responses to these questions can be generated as histograms (for a slider or slider with stones) or scatter plots (for a triad and canvas with stones) for the whole sample or for a subset of the sample dataset using The Cynefin Company's proprietary software or a third party solution. To more easily visualize dominant or strong patterns, and to differentiate them from outliers or weak signals, other types of two-dimensional density plots (such as distribution plots, contour maps, or heat maps) can be produced for triads and canvases with stones. These more elaborate graphs can be created with the Dashboard and Workbench, in the case of XY plots, or with R or Stata.

Once visualizations have been generated, it is good practice to document key observations with a brief description of the main pattern. Different versions of these visualizations can be produced; some may only contain the dots representing the responses, while others may include means or medians. In addition, during primary analysis, each signifier can be combined with specific filters or MCQ responses to make useful comparisons between subsets of responses. Based on the patterns detected during primary analysis, further inquiries and ideas for comprehensive analysis can then be identified.

It is important to keep in mind that a pattern is an entry point to explore the narratives in more depth. Their presence within a visualization offers insights into people's experiences, but they should not be interpreted by analysts or stakeholders as representing anything more than an initial reading of how the answers appear to be distributed. Patterns can become patterns of interest, to be followed up with more analysis, if they are considered surprising or significant enough for the learning questions to explore in more detail.

When stakeholders start identifying patterns, it may appear that the stories tagged to each data point have little in common, or that they 'should' have been tagged to a different pattern in a different area. It is important to remember that patterns are the result of respondents themselves tagging their stories to add new information to the narrative. Tagging is not a summary of what was shared in a story. Individual stories are snapshots of a given experience at a specific moment. Tagging adds additional layers of information to the narrative, rather than summarizing it.

Data points from slider, slider-with-stones, canvas-with-stones, and triad questions are captured as coordinates, which allows descriptive and statistical analysis (such as of correlations and statistical significance). This step is best when the sampling has followed statistically sound methods and the collection has successfully followed the sampling strategy.

Step 4: **Exploratory analysis of narratives**
Software used: Dashboard and Workbench, Tableau, R, NVivo, Atlas.ti

Analysis of narratives provides context to the descriptive and visual exploratory analysis. It helps to structure the content, identify commonly used terminology, and understand more about weak signals that show emergent trends or threats. It can also lead to surprising insights that fall outside the preidentified notions of the analytical framework, and that have thus not been embedded in the questions. Actively looking for 'unknown unknowns' (Mager et al. 2018) can reveal new problems that may need addressing, or new opportunities that can be supported.

This type of finding can shed new light on what matters to people and what affects their lives. While often only a limited number of narratives from the full set can be read by the people involved in sensemaking—especially if there are many hundreds of stories—they can point to critically important themes, such as divorce among young girls in Ethiopia (Girl Hub 2015), cyberbullying in Bangladesh (CARE, Tipping Point, 2017), or the effect that unpredictable or changing climate has on people's livelihoods and lives in a multi-country study aimed at understanding and assessing resilience (Gottret 2017).

Exploratory analysis of narratives can happen in different ways. Two possibilities during primary analysis include: (1) reading through narratives to spot respondent characteristics, decisions made, or actions taken in the experience; outcomes of the experience; influencers, supporters and, detractors; and other interesting elements or surprising aspects; and (2) looking at the frequency of words used and creating word clouds.

Guidance for visualizing and describing core SenseMaker signifier questions

The following sections provide guidance on how to visualize patterns from core SenseMaker signifier questions, and guiding questions and recommendations for properly describing them. In addition, concrete examples related to the different types and purposes of these questions are presented, in line with their description in the Design chapter.

The following recommendations for visualizing and describing the generated patterns apply to all types of signifier questions:

- Include the sample size with the visualization, as well as the counts and percentages of responses for the different subsets of the sample, describe the general pattern in combination with the available statistics (the median, mean, count, percentages, and percentiles), and any differences observed among subsets of responses.
- Include the original phrasing of the question with the visualization and refer to it in the description of the pattern.
- Highlight any interesting, surprising, or special patterns—including dominant patterns, outliers, and weak signals.
- Contextualize the description by extracting key insights from subsets of narratives for different groups of respondents (responses that fall around the median line and at the extremes, in the case of sliders and sliders with stones; and responses that fall in tight clusters, representing dominant responses, or in dispersed clusters, representing outliers or weak signals).

Analyzing slider signifier questions

Table 29 provides instructions and recommendations for analyzing slider signifier questions, while Table 30 illustrates some examples from practical SenseMaker processes that have been led by the authors.

A Practical Guide for Using SenseMaker

Table 29. Tips and recommendations for analyzing slider questions using The Cynefin Company's proprietary software

Types of plots	Responses can be visualized as dot plots, jitter plots, or histograms; a histogram is the most common and easiest way to visualize a slider.
Generating the visuals	Dashboard and Workbench enable the visualization of sliders as dot plots, jitter plots, and histograms, with the labels placed as they were entered into Designer. Workbench also includes options to add the mean, the median, and the distribution and normal distribution curves.
Understanding the visuals	When histograms are used to visualize sliders, the height of each bar represents the number of responses that were placed at that position on the slider. The position is captured as an X-coordinate value ranging from 0 to 100, with a 0 indicating that the position is at the extreme left, and a 100 indicating it is at the extreme right. It is usual to have an odd number of bars (columns) for the histogram, with one bar (column) representing the middle. The number of bars can be customized, widening or narrowing the range of responses (more bars provide more nuance).
Describing the visuals	The following questions are relevant for describing visuals generated from slider signifier questions: • How many respondents answered this question? • What is the overall pattern of responses (shape, center, spread) in relation to the two extremes on the slider? • What is the dominant pattern (strongest concentration of answers) and what is the deviation from the pattern (outliers)? • Does the distribution lean towards one of the extremes? Where is the median line? • How do overall patterns and deviations change for different subsets of the sample data? • What additional insights can we gain by analyzing narratives associated with responses near the median line or outliers? • What is surprising, whether by its absence or by its presence?

Table 30. Examples of types of slider signifier questions

Opposing extremes

Adolescent girls in Rwanda shared experiences of their daily life and indicated through this opposing negative slider question whether they were treated too harshly or too gently. The middle position suggests the ideal situation.

A closer investigation confirmed that the experiences in the middle were associated with positive feelings (proud, encouraged, and hopeful). Girls aged 16 to 19 years shared more stories of girls being treated harshly. Violence and insecurity were the main topics.

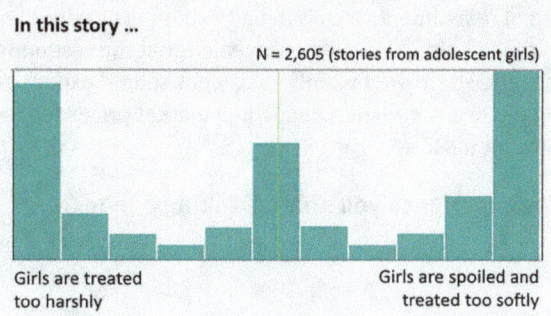

In this story ...

N = 2,605 (stories from adolescent girls)

Girls are treated too harshly — Girls are spoiled and treated too softly

Continuous scale

This slider was designed to assess the direction and extent of changes in income generated by participating only in marketing clubs (30.2% of project participants), only in savings and internal lending community (SILC) groups (55.3% of project participants), and in both types of groups (14.5% of project participants).

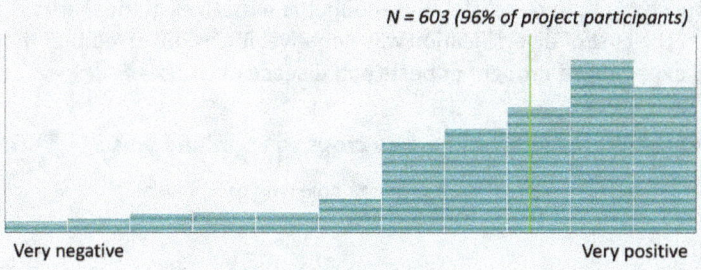

The experience you shared generated changes to your household income that were...

N = 603 (96% of project participants)

Very negative — Very positive

The responses show that, at the median (green line), project participants perceived a positive change in their income, with a strong concentration of responses to the right of the slider. However, some responses can also be observed close to the very negative extreme, showing that some project participants perceived negative changes in their income.

continued ⇢

Table 30 continued. Examples of types of slider signifier questions

Blending elements

77.5% of respondents who took a loan answered this signifier question. Responses leaned to the right, showing that, at the median, loans allowed respondents to improve their farming or expand their entrepreneurial activities. There was an outlier group of respondents that had bad experiences with their loans. Reading narratives from the left side of the slider revealed that the respondents had either used the money they borrowed mainly to pay household expenses, or they had invested in pigeon pea production and, when market prices fell severely, they suffered significant losses.

In the experience you shared, taking a loan...

N = 352 (77.5% of the sample who took a loan)

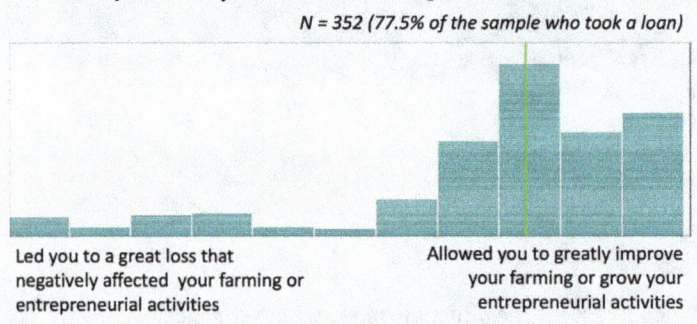

Led you to a great loss that negatively affected your farming or entrepreneurial activities

Allowed you to greatly improve your farming or grow your entrepreneurial activities

Different elements of a concept

Almost all respondents (96.6%) diversified their crops (by rotating or intercropping) and at the mean they considered that this practice was more beneficial than it was costly. This pattern was strong and dominant, and very few outliers considered that it was more costly than beneficial. By reading the narratives of those who considered that the cost of diversification was negative, it was observed that these producers had experienced drought or pests and disease of crops.

In the experience you shared, adding new crops to your land was...

N = 352 (77.5% of the sample who took a loan)

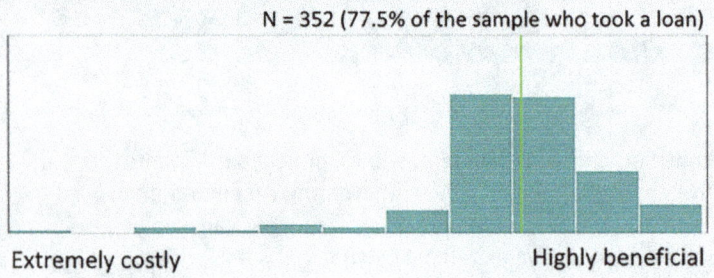

Extremely costly   Highly beneficial

Analyzing slider-with-stones signifier questions

The analysis of sliders with stones follows the same basic principles as the analysis of sliders, with a few differences. Table 31 provides instructions and recommendations for analyzing slider-with-stones signifier questions, while Table 32 illustrates some examples from SenseMaker processes led by the authors.

Table 31. Tips and recommendations for analyzing slider-with-stones questions using The Cynefin Company's proprietary software

Types of plots	Responses are usually visualized as a set of histograms separately representing responses to each 'stone', or response option. If these histograms are visualized on top of each other, they can allow valuable comparison between the responses to the different options included in the slider with stones.
Visualizing the responses	Dashboard and Workbench allow the visualization of sliders with stones as dot plots. However, the Y-axis has no meaning in this type of signifier question.
Understanding the visuals	The logic of interpretation is similar to that applied to slider questions. In addition, visualizing sliders with stones allows a comparison of response patterns of different response options or stones. It is also possible to use the count option to estimate the percentage of respondents that selected each option.
Describing the visuals	In addition to the questions provided to describe sliders in the previous section, the following questions are relevant in describing visuals generated from slider-with-stones signifier questions: • How many respondents selected each of the stones? What percentage of all respondents do these represent? • How do the histograms for the different options or stones compare in relation to their mean, median, distribution, shape, center, and spread? • How do the dominant patterns (strongest concentrations of answers) and the deviation from the patterns (outliers) vary between the histograms for the different stones? • Do overall patterns and deviations change for different subsets of the sample data? • What additional insights can we gain by analyzing the narratives associated with responses near the median line, and with outlying responses, for each histogram corresponding to each option or stone? • What is surprising by its absence or its presence?

Table 32. Examples of types of slider-with-stones signifier questions

Time-related stones

This slider with stones reconstructed the pathways followed by farm families in processes aimed at developing farmer competencies (organizational, financial, marketing, natural resource management, and innovation). The aim was to facilitate their engagement in markets, thus contributing to rural transformation.

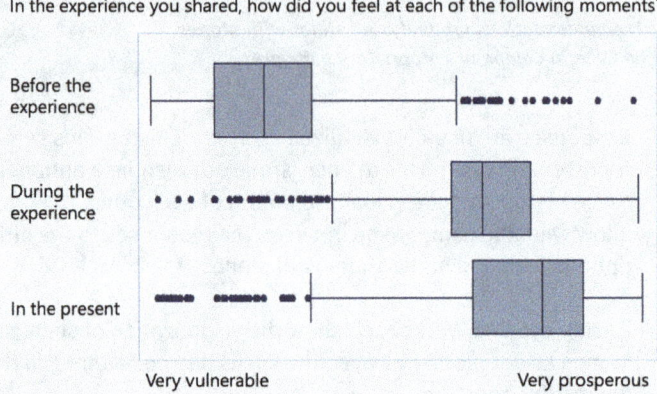

The results of all responses is shown in three boxplots, each representing a moment in the experience shared by respondents (before, during, and in the present). This series shows that, at the median (line within the boxes), farmers had progressed, initially faster and then slower. The spread of 50% of respondents around the median (responses along the box) was larger before the experience and in the present than during the experience. The spread of all respondents (respondents between the two whiskers, the horizontal lines) was also greater at present. Some outliers (the dots) showed farmers felt prosperous even before the experience, and others continued feeling vulnerable in the present. This slider with stones became the backbone for the assessment of the progress and resilience of farm families.

Actor-related stones

In a study assessing gender-related behavior change promoted by Community Conversation Groups (CCG), this slider with stones was used to assess: (1) who motivated community members to change their behavior, and (2) the extent to which these different influencers (family members or relatives, community members, traditional or religious leaders, CCG members, leaders from other community organizations, government workers and NGO workers) committed to support them.

The boxplots for each influencer show that respondents at the median (line within the boxes) perceived that all these influencers were committed to support them, with the most committed being NGO workers (median nearer the right extreme).

continued ⇢

Table 32 continued. Examples of types of slider-with-stones signifier questions

Half the respondents were motivated to change their behavior by CCG members, perceived as very committed at the median. Responses were less spread out (shorter distance between the two whiskers) and the two outliers were only in the center of the slider.

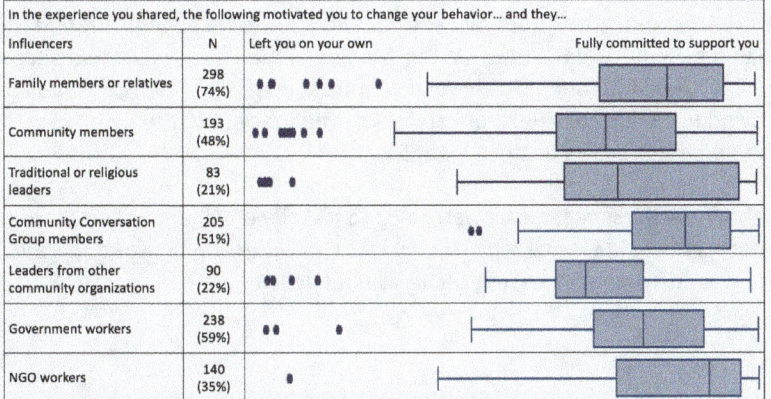

This finding was important to assess who motivated gender-related behavior change and their commitment to support community members to change their behaviors. This refines program design to improve the effectiveness of behavior change promotion efforts.

Practice-related and outcome-related stones

In a baseline assessment of resilience conducted in the Democratic Republic of the Congo, this slider with stones was used to identify transformative strategies catalyzed by recent shocks and stressors that people had experienced (armed conflict, social and political conflict, disease, and climate change). It also assessed the extent to which these strategies were negatively or positively transforming people's lives.

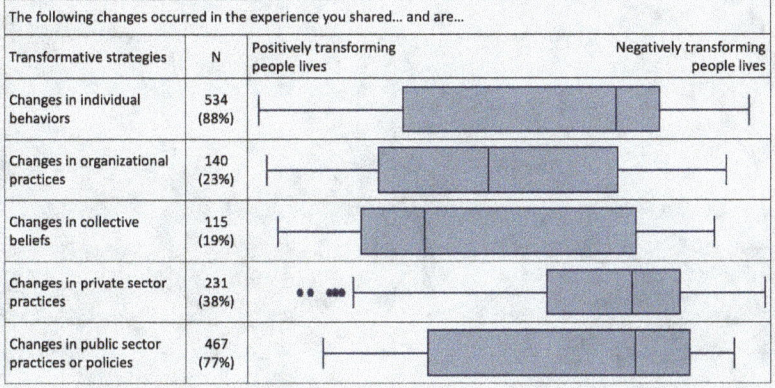

A Practical Guide for Using SenseMaker

The series of five boxplots highlights that more respondents perceived changes in individual behaviors and public sector practices and policies, and that these changes were negatively transforming people's lives at the median (line within the box towards the right extreme). But responses were very spread along the boxes (50% of responses) and between the two whiskers (encompassing all responses). This was also the case with private sector practices, although fewer respondents reported these changes. Some outliers (dots on the left side of the slider) indicate responses about positive transformation. Fewer respondents saw changes in organizational practices and in collective beliefs, but still perceived these are positively transforming people's lives to some extent.

The insights from these responses were used to identify emergent practices within the program that could strengthen changes in organizational practices and collective beliefs, and reduce negative changes in individual behaviors.

Analyzing canvas-with-stones signifier questions

The analysis of a canvas with stones follows the same basic principles and approach to the exploratory analysis of the slider-with-stones questions, with a few differences. Table 33 provides instructions and recommendations for analyzing canvas-with-stones signifier questions, and Table 34 illustrates some examples from SenseMaker processes led by the authors.

Table 33. Tips and recommendations for analyzing canvas-with-stones signifier questions using The Cynefin Company's proprietary software

Types of plots	Responses are usually visualized as a scatter plot with an X-axis and Y-axis for each stone; however, they can also be visualized as two related histograms for the level of analysis, similar to that of the slider-with-stones signifier questions. In addition, other types of two-dimensional density plots (such as distribution plots, contour plots, or heat maps) can also be used to better visualize dominant or strong patterns and to differentiate them from weak signals.
Visualizing the responses	Dashboard and Workbench automatically visualize canvases with stones as dot plots, allowing insight into where the responses lay within this canvas for each option or stone. In addition, the XY plot option allows these visualizations to be customized by adding trend lines and representing dots with contour maps.
Understanding the visuals	The logic of interpretation of the canvas-with-stones signifier questions is similar to that for sliders and slider-with-stones questions. Each dot on the canvas represents a data point, and may be tightly clustered or form a pattern, such as a line or a contour map, thus showing trends, dominant patterns, and weak signals. It is also possible to compare the responses for different options or stones on the canvas. Unique about a canvas-with-stones signifier question is that it can visualize associations or relationships between the two dimensions that form either side of the canvas.
Describing the visuals	In addition to the questions provided to describe sliders and sliders with stones in the previous sections, the following questions are also useful to describe visuals generated from canvas-with-stones questions: • How many respondents selected all of the stones? What percentage of all respondents do these represent? • What is the overall pattern of responses? Is there a high concentration of dots in one place, or are the dots evenly spread across the plot? • What is the overall pattern of responses for each response option? • Is there a deviation from the pattern (outliers)? • Do overall patterns and deviations change for different subsets of the sample data? • What additional insights can we gain by analyzing narratives associated with specific dominant clusters or outliers? • What is surprising by its absence or its presence?

Table 34. Examples of types of canvas-with-stones signifier questions

In the experience you shared, how do you see the natural resources on your plot of land?

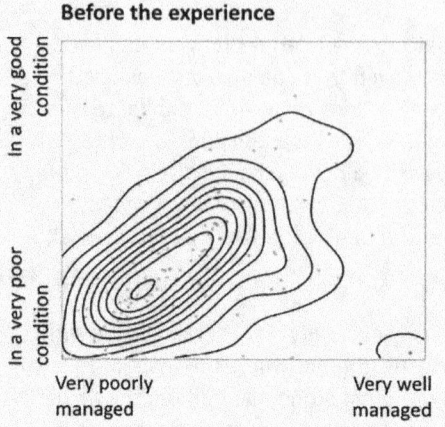
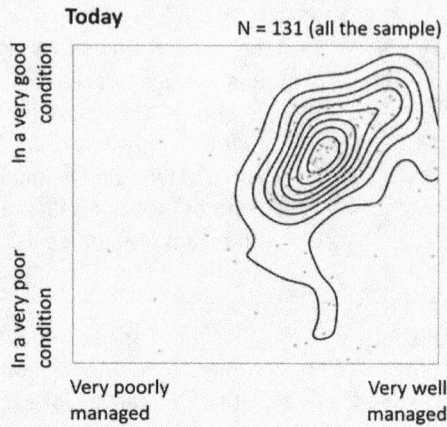

N = 131 (all the sample)

Time-and resource-related stones

This canvas with stones was designed to assess changes in the health of an ecosystem, as well as the influence of users in the management of different natural resources that were given as options or stones.

These examples are from a study conducted by CRS in Guatemala to assess changes in competencies and behaviors as a result of training, coaching, and mentoring activities aimed at developing farmers' competencies to manage the soil and water resources on their land, to restore and protect them, and improve their land's productivity.

These visualizations were generated using the XY plot function in Analyst (now called Dashboard and Workbench) and the 'landscape' option to generate a two-dimensional contour plot. The visualization for the water resources before the experience and now shows that most respondents perceived water resources have been in poor condition and poorly managed before the experience. In the present, most respondents perceived that they are now being well-managed with improvement in their condition. The same pattern can be observed for soil resources but with perceptions of the current soil condition still dispersed. Responses had shifted from the poorly managed side to the well-managed one.

These perceptions provided positive feedback on the effectiveness of the program, not only in building water and soil management competencies, but on the outcomes of these improved competencies. It is important to understand that these are the perceptions of respondents, and not quantitative measurements of the condition of the natural resources. The program could combine these results with quantitative data to validate these perceptions or, if findings of the two methods differed, the program could seek to create awareness of the real condition of these resources.

Actor-related stones

This canvas with stones was designed to give insight into how people perceived the commitment (or willingness) and power of important local actors to change the situations described in the narratives.

In this example, from a baseline study conducted by CRS for a peacebuilding project in Mindanao, Philippines, respondents were asked to indicate how much power and commitment local actors had to improve the situation shared in the story. These visualizations were generated for each of the local actors (stones) with the contour map function in SenseMaker Workbench.

These contour maps show the power/commitment grid for each local actor. While the military and police had clear power and high commitment to improving the situation, communities—including traditional and religious leaders—had more situations in which they seemed to be powerless, although their commitment to resolve the situation was high.

Each graph can be further controlled by geographical area or type of conflict to gain more context-specific insights into how people perceived the role of local actors in changing the situation.

In your story the following actor has the ...

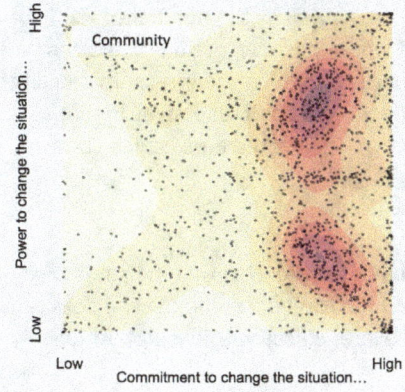

In your story the following actor has the ...

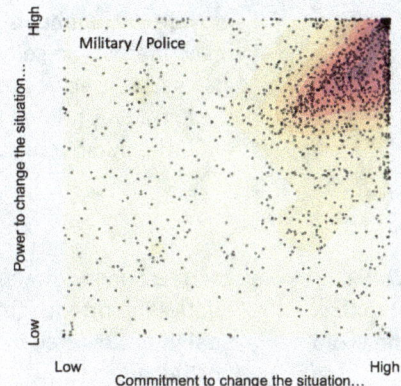

Analyzing triad signifier questions

Triad signifier questions are quite different in nature from the other types of signifier question. Guidance and recommendations for analyzing and interpreting triad questions are shown in Table 35. Tables 36 and 37 illustrate examples of visualizing and interpreting triad signifier questions from SenseMaker processes led by the authors. The examples show different ways of visualizing triads. The patterns in the triads are represented by using dots, zone percentages, distribution plots, heat maps (contour fill) and by indicating the mean in the triad.

Table 35. Tips and recommendations for analyzing triad questions using The Cynefin Company's proprietary software

Types of plots	Responses are visualized as triangular graphs, also known as ternary plots or trilinear plots. Triads can also be visualized using different types of two-dimensional density plots (distribution plots, contour plots, or heat maps) to better visualize dominant or strong patterns and to differentiate them from weak signals.
Visualizing the responses	Each response corresponds to a dot in the triad that is plotted using the X and Y coordinates in the dataset. Dashboard and Workbench automatically visualize triads and provide the number of responses, as well as the number of respondents who selected the 'not applicable' option. Users can also select specific areas of the triad and analyze further by reading the narratives related to the specific group of responses in that area. The number of responses in the selected area is also shown.
Understanding the visuals	Each response corresponds to a dot in the triad that indicates the relative importance (balance) of the three elements. These dots can be tightly clustered in one or several places within a plot, or loosely positioned. The closer a dot is to a corner, the stronger is the presence of that element in the concept, and the weaker the other two elements are. The relative importance of each element in the triad is captured by a value that ranges from 0 to 100, indicating how close the dot is to the corner. The higher the value, the closer the dot is to the respective corner. Dots located exactly in one corner mean that only one element (the one in that corner) was present in the story and the value for this element is thus 100, and the other two elements take the value 0.

Understanding the visuals	A dot located on the edge of the triangle—located part way between two elements—means that the third element was not present. The value for the element that is not present is 0, and the values for the two that are present will sum to 100.

Dots located inside the triad and not touching any of the corners or lines mean that all three elements of the concept were present in the respondent's experience. In this case, each of the three elements will have a nonzero value, depending on its relative importance, and the values of the three elements will add up to 100.

Responses in the middle may mean different things – the presence of each of the three concepts was equally strong, or the presence of each was equally weak.

The position of each dot is not absolute; it is relative. It is thus extremely important to interpret a response pattern relative to all three concepts, and not just one.

A response of 'not applicable' means that none of the elements of the concept assessed by the triad were present, which is itself a finding. Depending on the triad and the elements of the concept evaluated, this may even be a desirable response—for example, in a triad that assesses the relative importance of three constraints or negative elements. |
| **Describing the visuals** | The following questions will help describe the responses to triad signifier questions:

- How many respondents answered this question? What percentage do they represent of the total sample?
- What is the overall pattern of responses (high concentration of dots in one place or evenly spread across the plot)? What does this mean with respect to the relative importance of the three elements of the triad?
- Is there a deviation from the pattern (outliers representing weak signals)? What percentage of respondents are in this area of the triad? What does it mean with respect to the relative importance of the three elements of the triad?
- Do overall patterns and deviations change for different subsets of the sample data?
- What additional insights can we gain by analyzing the narratives associated with specific clusters or outliers?
- What is surprising by its absence or its presence? |

Table 36. Examples of analyzing different triad signifier questions

Exploration of a concept

This triad was developed to assess behavior change as a result of financial education. There were no assumptions for specific patterns of responses. As the program aimed to support livelihood development, it was considered desirable if more savings were used for farming or entrepreneurial activities, and part of the savings used for household expenses and setting up an emergency fund.

In this figure, the dots represent the position of the respective stories and generate the pattern in the triad. The triad shows that 94% of respondents used their savings for any of these purposes (their dots are in the triad). This is already an important gain for the program, as it means that not only were project participants saving (main behavioral evidence), but they were also using their savings for the hoped-for purposes.

The high concentration of dots near the upper tip shows that respondents are using more of their savings for investing in their farming or entrepreneurial activities, followed by paying household expenses (bottom left) and, to a lesser extent, to respond to emergencies (bottom right).

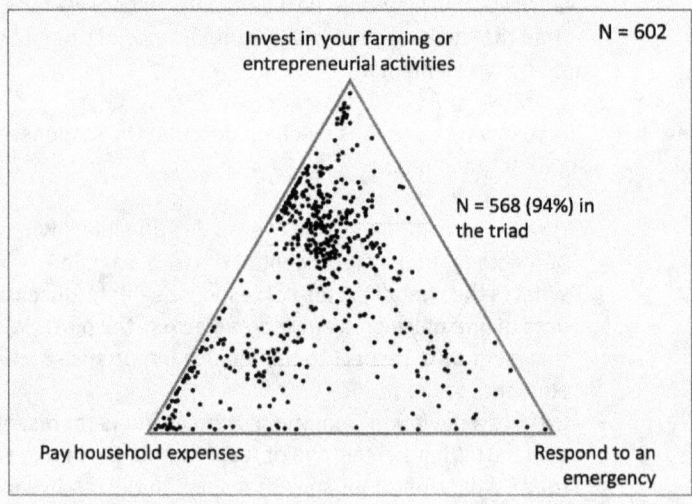

In the experience you shared, you used more of your savings to...

- Invest in your farming or entrepreneurial activities
- N = 602
- N = 568 (94%) in the triad
- Pay household expenses
- Respond to an emergency

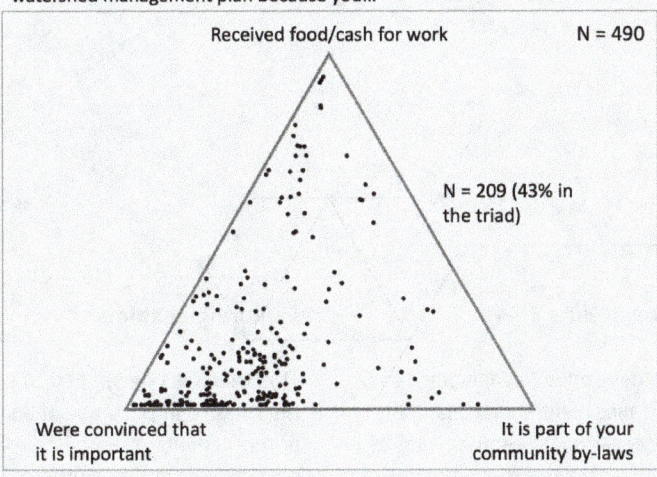

In the experience you shared, you committed to the implementation of the watershed management plan because you...

Testing an assumption

This triad was developed to test program assumptions about building and institutionalizing the value of conservation. One of the assumptions was that if communities collectively designed and implemented watershed management plans and members started to see positive change, they would continue to implement action to restore and protect their watersheds because they would be convinced of its importance and not only because they were given food or cash for work. As people started seeing its importance, it would also become a formal norm embedded in community by-laws.

The figure shows dots representing the position given by respondents about their stories. The triad shows that only 43% of respondents lived in a community that had (or knew about) a watershed management plan. As this program was midway through implementation, this alone was an important achievement but needed to be scaled to other communities.

For those respondents (n=209) whose community had a watershed management plan, the strong pattern in the bottom left corner shows that the main reason for committing to its implementation was their conviction about its importance, validating the first assumption. A light cluster of responses linked people's motivation to plans being part of community by-laws. Given these responses, the program team now aimed for more responses at the center in the bottom part of the triad. This would show that community members find it important as well as it being part of community by-laws.

A more in-depth analysis of the narratives located in the upper tip may give ideas about what the program might do to reduce these responses further.

Table 36. Examples of analyzing different triad signifier questions

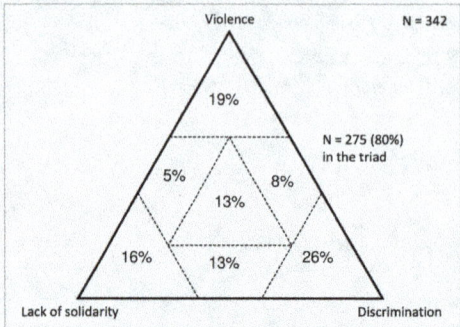

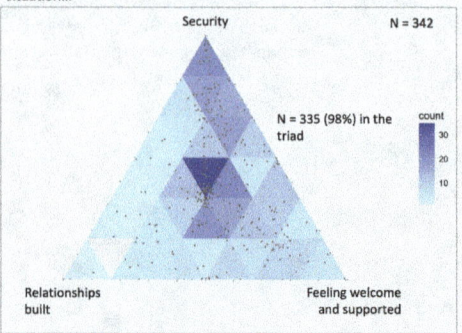

Exploring constraints

This triad was developed to understand the relative importance of different constraints faced by refugees when integrating into their host communities, and to explore options of how a program could reduce the main barriers to their integration. The expectation was that interventions would reduce the number of responses that fell inside this triad (Gottret and Kast 2018).

This figure shows the percentage of responses in each of the zones in the triad and was generated using the SenseMaker Workbench. It shows that 80% of refugees experienced a combination of discrimination, violence and lack of solidarity (responses inside the triad). The highest percentage of respondents (26%) experienced mainly discrimination, followed by 19% who experienced mainly violence, and 16% mainly lack of solidarity, while 13% experienced all three constraints equally, and 13% a combination of discrimination and lack of solidarity. This shows that while the three factors affected negatively their recovery, discrimination was perceived by respondents to be the strongest of the three barriers.

Filtering this triad by gender showed important differences. While discrimination was found to be the greater challenge for most men, women reported that all three challenges were equally challenging for them.

Exploring enablers

This triad was developed to understand the relative importance of enablers of refugee integration, and to explore options for amplifying them. The expectation was that interventions would increase the number of responses that fell in this triad (Gottret and Kast 2018).

This visualization was generated in R using a distribution plot. The darker the area, the higher the concentration of dots (responses) in that area.

In this example, the triad shows that 98% of respondents reported experiencing an enabling factor to integrate in their host communities. Feeling secure, followed by feeling welcome and supported, was more helpful in overcoming the experience shared by respondents, with the relationships built reported as less enabling.

Filtering this triad by gender showed important differences. The three enablers tended to have a similar importance for men, while women assigned more significance to feeling secure, welcome, and supported, than to the relationships built.

Table 37. Examples of context-specific and generic triad signifier questions

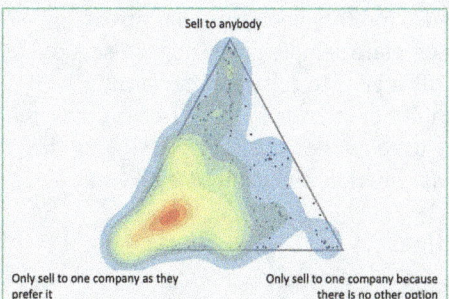
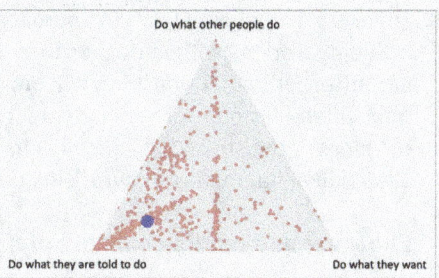

Context-specific triad

This triad was used in an Inclusive Business Scan tool (Deprez and Van den Steen 2016) to understand the trading relationships between smallholder farmers and their buyers, specifically looking at farmers' loyalty to and dependency on buyers.

The visualization for this triad is a heatmap generated in SenseMaker Workbench. It uses the contour map function to show the areas where there are a greater concentration of responses (in red and orange), some concentration of responses (in green), and fewer responses (in blue).

This example shows the results of an assessment conducted for the cacao value chain in Indonesia. It indicates that most farmers leaned toward selling their produce to a single company, because they preferred to cooperate with it. However, a substantial number of farmers (more than 20%) also sold to anybody, mostly because they lived in areas where there was a strong presence of powerful middlemen who regularly offered higher prices. This situation, combined with the remoteness of the area, made the support services offered by the company less effective.

Generic triad

This triad was used to assess the effects of vocational and technical training in the lives and livelihoods of vulnerable youth, as part of a youth empowerment program.

The visualization for this triad, generated using the SenseMaker Workbench, shows each response as a dot. The larger blue dot is the mean and shows that young people are more inclined to do what they are told to do.

This example shows that, in the majority of the situations described in the stories, young people did what they were told to do regarding the issues related to their education and professional life. Parents, teachers, and employers had a significant influence in the life of vulnerable youth. The cluster of stories where the youth did what they wanted came mainly from students in their final year of training. This subgroup felt they could make decisions about the type of courses and future work, relationships, and moving out of home. Interestingly, the stories from youth who were already working showed the strongest tendency to doing what they were told.

Guidance for reading and analyzing narratives

There are a number of ways to approach the exploratory analysis of narratives, including working with narratives from the complete sample, analyzing subsets of narratives, or both. Doing both will provide the means to compare the narratives from different groups of respondents. The choice of subsets of narratives is driven by the focus of the study, the analytical framing used as the basis for its design, or the detection of interesting or surprising patterns, whether dominant or weak.

Choosing and reading subsets of narratives

Narratives may be grouped by responses to sociodemographic multiple-choice questions (such as comparing women's narratives with men's); or by responses to signifier MCQs (such as comparing narratives signified by respondents as negative, neutral, or positive). For example, in a girls' empowerment program focused on ending child marriage, the team was able to analyze in more depth narratives from girls that related their experiences to the theme of marriage; or from girls who related their experiences to different feelings, such as happiness, pride, worry, or sadness. Narratives were also used to contrast girls' experiences that they tagged as 'happening frequently' with those they tagged as 'rare'. In another example, involving a value chain program, an initial reading exercise took place with NGO staff members, buyers, and government officials, focusing on narratives from smallholder farmer respondents who tagged their experiences as 'negative' and those who tagged them as 'positive'.

Narratives can also be analyzed in a subset of responses from those who placed their answers in different areas of a slider, a slider with stones, a canvas with stones, or a triad. The last of these involves reading the narratives of those respondents who placed their responses in dominant patterns (areas with many responses) or narratives of those respondents who were outliers (in areas with few responses). SenseMaker explicitly values and enables the examination outliers. A cluster of outliers within a slider, a slider with stones, a canvas with stones, or a triad that deviates from the dominant pattern of responses may be a sign of an unexpected

---

Box 11.

Difficult life conditions – a narrative from a female agricultural worker in northern Africa

My colleague became pregnant but, wanting to work, she always put a band around her stomach to hide the pregnancy, and presented a fake medical certificate. But the boss was told by another colleague, and he insulted and humiliated her in front of everybody and fired her without pity, even though she really needed the work because her husband wasn't working (Mager et al. 2018).

subgroup experiencing a particular issue. Looking at the narratives related to that outlier cluster or weak signal can help shed light on the underlying issues or the context from which such experiences emerge. This is important, as it can help identify situations or practices that a program may want to encourage, or concerns or problems that may need mitigation.

Another way to select subsets of narratives is to search for those that contain a specific word. For example, in a study conducted to understand agricultural workers' experiences (Mager et al. 2018), a subset of narratives was identified by running a word search for several pregnancy-related keywords, such as 'pregnancy', 'pregnant', and 'birth'. A qualitative analysis of this small set of narratives (see Box 11) uncovered the negative treatment of pregnant women by their supervisors. This revealed how the well-being of pregnant workers was being compromised by the physical demands of their jobs and by harassment from superiors. Pregnant women also attempted to hide their pregnancy for as long as possible, due to the precarious nature of their employment, knowing that workers who became pregnant were often fired.

Analyzing narratives

Narratives can be analyzed by reading the selected groups of narratives and extracting elements of interest. For example, using a slider with time-related stones, respondents were categorized into three groups: those who followed a prosperous pathway, those who followed a resilient pathway, and those who followed a vulnerable pathway. To contrast these three types of respondents, groups of narratives from each category were read in order to determine the personal characteristics and capabilities of responses in each group, the support they received, whether they faced shocks or stressors (and if so, what kind), the actions they took to cope with the events; the steps they took to adapt; the transformational changes present in the story; and livelihood outcomes. This enabled the identification of the actions, responses, and transformational changes that a program might want to amplify to build resilience, as well as of the actions, responses, and changes that a program might want to address in order to reduce the number of respondents following vulnerable pathways in the future.

Narratives can also be analyzed by answering the following questions:
- What aspects seem to recur in most narratives of a selected subset (e.g. tagged as negative) compared to those selected from a different subset (e.g. tagged as positive)?
- What might this tell us about what helps or hinders the situation? Does this relate to certain events, certain relationships, or certain conditions?

Figure 15. Visualizing the most frequently used words

- What attitudes, behaviors, actions, and responses can be observed that made the difference between these subsets of narratives?

Another way to analyze narratives is to use word clouds, which are graphic representations of word frequency. The larger the word in the plot, the more common the word occurs in the narratives. Word clouds can help to identify words that frequently appear in a set of narratives. They are a simple way to compare words used by different subsets of respondents to describe the same issue, and are helpful when communicating themes and insights to stakeholders. Word clouds can be created for narratives from the overall sample or for a specific subset. This type of analysis enables the identification of the most common and least common words, which may give additional ideas about what to explore during comprehensive analysis.

For example, word counts and word clouds were generated using the narratives of producers whose trajectories over time followed a prosperous path, a resilient pathway, and a vulnerable pathway in a study conducted to evaluate the CRS Farmer-to-Farmer program in Kenya (Gottret et al. 2017).

The word cloud generated from the narratives of farmers who followed prosperous pathways (Figure 15) shows that some of the words mentioned most often in these narratives were related to agriculture and small livestock production ('farming', 'planted', 'production', 'harvest', 'maize', and 'chicken'); showed positive change ('good', 'able', 'helped', 'decided'); described outcomes ('money', 'school', 'fees', 'income', 'food', 'life', and 'land'), and were centered on family and children.

Building Block 2: Collective Interpretation

Interpretation of primary analysis findings can be undertaken by a single person, the core team, or with key stakeholders identified during the Preparation phase. Collective interpretation events provide important opportunities to include stakeholders whose voices were left out during the collection process, groups of respondents, facilitators and, most importantly, the people who will be using the findings in their daily work to improve programming design and implementation, and those who need to make strategic decisions.

SenseMaker is very well suited for collective interpretation. The visual patterns make it easy for anyone to visualize the findings, and to engage in discussions to interpret them collectively. This feature of the method can strongly contribute to the uptake of findings, by building wider analytical capacity and, in the process, informing decision-making and action.

Benefits of involving key stakeholders

Involving key stakeholders in the collective interpretation of findings from primary analysis has a number of benefits.

It improves the depth, quality, and robustness of sensemaking. Different people bring different experiences and expertise to the table when they look at the findings. Diverse stakeholder perspectives add layers of meaning and new interpretations, and raise different questions for further inquiry. Their input significantly improves the nature of the findings and confidence in them.

It supports accountability. When SenseMaker is used for evaluative studies, reflection with people involved in implementation encourages them to be accountable for the quality and impact of their own work. Where it is possible to engage public donors, civil society organizations, and the private sector in collective interpretation, this can validate observations and support decisions on strategic priorities. Yet the most powerful form of accountability occurs when reflections happen with intended project participants: These opportunities allow them to assess what has been achieved (or not), how they contributed to these achievements, and the changes they need to make or actions they need to take to improve their own lives.

It promotes learning and use of findings at different levels. By collectively discussing what findings are saying, learning is embedded with those who can act on insights. Talking through what they mean to different stakeholders, and their implications for action, shortens the distance between the findings and them being taken up by their intended audience. Such discussions can cover how to deal with challenges faced but, for this to happen, clear objectives and the involvement of the right people are essential.

Agreeing on the objectives of collective interpretation

Before investing in collective interpretation, the core team will need to decide if it is necessary to achieve the original purpose of the SenseMaker process. If it is, then it is important to clarify the objectives of collective interpretation and how they will be achieved. Examples of common objectives are presented in Table 38 and include:

- sharing findings from the primary analysis with key stakeholders;
- collecting different perspectives and insights on the findings from stakeholders to improve the analysis, interpretation, and contextualization;
- identifying topics and questions for further analysis, comprehensive analysis, or exploration of weak signals and surprising patterns;
- promoting collective reflection for project adaptation and strategic decision-making for further implementation;
- contributing to program strategy design and implementation;
- promoting broader ownership of findings to influence change processes;
- inspiring and creating insights to imagine a new future and to act; and
- stimulating collaboration among stakeholders.

Decisions need to be made about how to conduct and prepare for collective interpretation, including who to involve and how to involve them, what activities are needed, and how to sequence them. There is no one-size-fits-all recommendation. It all depends on the context of the SenseMaker process: location, available human and financial resources, available time, and the willingness of stakeholders to invest time. Table 38 summarizes a range of examples of the collective interpretation process, with their objectives and steps.

Table 38. Examples of different ways to structure collective interpretation

SENSEMAKER PROCESS PURPOSE	OBJECTIVES OF COLLECTIVE INTERPRETATION
Review of progress in ethical trading in a value chain in an African country (Oxfam, ETI, anonymized to protect current project efforts)	• Assess organizational potential for greater use of SenseMaker. • Show potential of SenseMaker to go beyond existing audit processes. • Present and validate initial findings. • Identify possible reasons for key observations, particularly surprising ones.
Evaluation of ten years of the Population, Refugees and Migration project, which sought to assess refugees' well-being and their social and economic integration in reception communities (CRS, Ecuador)	• Collect perspectives and insights on the findings of a final evaluation. • Position and influence future programming design and implementation as part of handing over a project to other organizations. • Influence donor approach and investment.
Action research into the functioning of a national network of social organizations and tourist providers, aimed at making holidays possible for people in poverty (Flanders, Belgium)	• Present, validate, and conduct further analysis; interpret findings. • Share key findings and formulate concrete recommendations for the future.
Measure and understand the inclusiveness of smallholder supply chains to create an understanding of the main bottlenecks, opportunities, and possible means for improvement. Inclusive Business Scan: coffee, cacao and rice value chains (VECO/Rikolto International in DRC, Indonesia, Nicaragua and Senegal)	• Conduct primary analysis and interpret results. • Discuss primary analysis, conduct further analysis, and read narratives around five inclusive business principles. • Facilitate interactive pattern discussions and narrative reading to identify the main bottlenecks, opportunities, and concrete actions. • Propose collaborative actions among value chain actors.

continued ⇢

WHO WAS INVOLVED	HOW IT WAS CONDUCTED
• ETI and Oxfam staff • Lead researchers (Oxfam and consultant)	**Step 1:** Two-day meeting with lead researchers and the core team to identify main patterns **Step 2:** One-day session with ETI to share and discuss **Step 3:** Half-day session with ETI and buyers to identify key problems that needed more effort
• Project team (CRS and partners) • Selected facilitators • Country and regional program leadership • Peer governmental and nongovernmental organizations • Donor staff	**Step 1:** Two-day workshop with the project team (CRS and partners) **Step 2:** One-day workshop with key stakeholders
• Program staff • All actors in the network • Pool of facilitators	**Step 1:** Two-day workshop with program staff (12 people) to carry out a first collective interpretation following the primary analysis **Step 2:** One-day sensemaking conference with all 30 facilitators (people who carried out in-depth collection of 500 stories in a six month period) **Step 3:** Two-hour presentation of results to the national forum of the network (400 people) **Step 4:** Half-day workshop with 50 representatives of the network
• 40 representatives of farmers and technical and management staff of the farmer organizations • Representatives of the buyers, all relevant value chain supporters or influencers	**Step 1:** One-week primary analysis and collective interpretation event with core team **Step 2:** Two-day interpretation meeting with program staff **Step 3:** Two-day sensemaking workshop at farmer organization level with forty representative farmers **Step 4:** One-day collective workshop with all stakeholders of the value chain with farmers, staff of farmer organizations, buyers, government actors, service providers, and financial institutions *continued* ⸺⟶

Phase 4: Sensemaking

Table 38. Examples of different ways to structure collective interpretation

SENSEMAKER PROCESS PURPOSE	OBJECTIVES OF COLLECTIVE INTERPRETATION
Conduct a baseline study on resilience for the Prepared and Resilient project as part of disaster risk reduction programming in Southeast Asia (CRS in Indonesia, Bangladesh, and Timor-Leste)	• Conduct collective analysis and interpretation of findings. • Triangulate analysis and interpret associations and correlations. • Collect different perspectives and insights into the findings of the baseline assessment. • Propose ideas to refine project design and implementation.
Conduct a baseline study for the A3B peacebuilding program on Mindanao Island, Philippines, and draw lessons and recommendations for improving program interventions (CRS, Philippines)	• Analyze the observed patterns, guided by the analysis framework. • Present the main findings and conduct further in-depth interpretation of the key dimensions of the analysis framework. • Formulate concrete actions and recommendations to improve program design.

Considerations for facilitating collective interpretation

As with any interpretation process, good preparation and facilitation are important. Being clear on who will facilitate any of the joint sensemaking sessions is important, in particular to ensure that someone with significant prior analytical experience with SenseMaker is available.

Participation

The initial stakeholder analysis from the Preparation phase (Table 4) is a useful resource for determining who should ideally be involved. Thinking about the number of participants is important, although there is no ideal size. Combining primary analysis with training in SenseMaker makes small groups of no more than five or six desirable. For collective interpretation with respondents, facilitators and implementing staff, a group of 15 to 20 participants can be easily managed. For events in which more in-depth collective interpretation is expected, a smaller group of 10 to 15 participants may be sufficient.

Event sequence and design

Collective interpretation is often not a one-off event involving all stakeholders, as Table 38 shows. It can be made up of multiple, well-sequenced events. For example, an event could be organized with program-related stakeholders to prepare initial findings. These could then be interpreted in a forum of a more diverse group of stakeholders. If power issues could hinder open discussion, it might be best to

WHO WAS INVOLVED	HOW IT WAS CONDUCTED
• Project teams and country program heads of programming	**Step 1:** Four- to five-day interpretation workshops with project teams in each country
• Program staff • Local partner NGOs from the five municipalities on Mindanao Island participating in the program	**Step 1:** Three-day collective analysis and interpretation workshop with the core program staff, including basic training in SenseMaker analysis **Step 2:** Three-day participatory interpretation workshops with the implementing local partner NGOs

organize parallel or sequential sessions with different groups. Table 38 gives examples of how different stakeholders were grouped for collective interpretation events, and how analysis events were sequenced to meet their objectives. Beginning the collective interpretation with the intended project participants can be very useful, as their insights can be incorporated in subsequent presentations to program and partner teams and leadership. However, it may also be desirable to conduct a collective interpretation event with only the analysis team, or with selected staff, in order to initially create a safe space in which to discuss emerging findings and ask tough questions, before bringing in other stakeholders.

Once key stakeholders are identified and linked to an optimal set of events, their content, agenda, and length can be developed. Consider how the findings and outputs of one collective interpretation event can inform another event. Plan enough time between events to document outputs and prepare for the next event. To determine the content of each event, consider the following questions:

- What would participants want to take away from this event, in order to feel that it was worthwhile?
- What do they already know about the SenseMaker process (and which therefore does not need to be covered in depth during the event)?
- What needs to be achieved to facilitate collaborative learning and to inform decisions and actions based on the findings?
- What findings from any primary analysis will be of greatest interest to them, and might fuel their curiosity about what else the data could say?

The discussions of the core team around these questions can then be organized as in Table 39 below. If possible, meet with the different stakeholders to understand their expectations and interests. Asking them how the findings might be useful for them, and what they want to achieve by participating in these events will provide important information for planning successful events.

Another important consideration when deciding on the content and length of events, and of the sessions within the events, is that stakeholders are likely to be more interested in the findings rather than in the SenseMaker method. Although a basic knowledge of the interpretation method used is useful, prioritize presentation of findings and, above all, discuss findings.

Content preparation

Once the focus and sequence of each event is clear, any preliminary findings from the primary analysis that will be shared are now prepared. Formats may include annotated presentations, flip charts or printed posters, handouts and briefs. This primary analysis stage does not justify investing in detailed reports, as the collective interpretation will provide rich content for a final report.

If those conducting primary analysis are still being trained in SenseMaker analysis, a skilled SenseMaker practitioner can help by reviewing the data that will be used for the presentation and indicating how this can be conveyed as clearly as possible. It is useful to be clear what will guide the presentation: the anchor concepts, the learning questions, or analytical ideas.

Table 39. Template for planning the content of collective interpretation events

Event	Stakeholders invited	Information of interest to the stakeholder	Findings to be presented	Session in which the findings will be presented

Story packs are best prepared ahead of time, as they must be selected with care, which is time-consuming. The story packs that are selected should provide the most impact. Fewer is better than too many. Consider the following:

- Do not include narratives of respondents who did not give their consent to share them.
- Include some demographic information and responses to selected follow-up questions, in order to give more information on the profile of the respondent and the experience shared.
- Do not include any details that could be used to identify the person (such as name or address), especially if confidentiality was assured as part of consent.
- Anonymize any information that might compromise the process or individuals, such as negative opinions about specific staff, the community or producer organizations, government staff, or politicians.
- Photos of respondents or facilitators should only be used with their explicit consent and where people are not put at risk; they should never be linked directly to a story. Credit must also be given to the photographer.

Facilitation process

Collective interpretation is most effective when well-organized, clean, user-friendly inputs are provided, when provocative questions are raised, and when participants are encouraged to freely engage in discussion. Facilitators need to become almost invisible, available only to guide participants through discovering key findings. Clustering initial findings helps in preparing short, engaging presentations that can lead into group and plenary discussions. For collective interpretation with project or program staff, the analytical framework used for the SenseMaker process can inform the organization of the findings.

When facilitating collective interpretation with key stakeholders to influence decision-making and action, try to select up to six main preliminary messages or insights generated during primary analysis likely to be of greatest interest to the invited stakeholders. These key messages can then be organized in sessions and ordered in a sequence that tells a story. A good practice is to start with the second-most important message, in order to capture the attention of respondents, and then end with the most important message—the one that will lead to crucial decisions and actions.

Some recommendations on how to structure the flow of the sessions are provided below.

Step 1. **Focus on the learning questions and participants' assumptions**

Start by reminding the participants of the purpose of the session and the learning question that will be explored using the SenseMaker data. Collect participants' assumptions about what they think will emerge as key findings.

Step 2. **Engage participants with the key findings**

Present the findings in a manner that engages participants and reflects their assumptions. Usually this implies providing the necessary amount of information, followed by a collective discussion that contrasts the findings with the assumptions. The kinds of questions that can be used include:

- What do you think are the responses of the average respondent, or of most respondents? Why?
- Why do think most respondents would give this answer?
- How do your assumptions compare with the actual data?

Step 3. **Reflect on key findings, review assumptions, and identify main conclusions**

Allocate sufficient time to interpret patterns, to read the story packs, to reflect on or validate the assumptions supported by the evidence, to challenge and discard any assumptions not supported by the evidence, and to embrace new assumptions. What information shows that the existing strategies and practices are effective, and which ones might be problematic? What gaps are exposed in people's thinking and activities?

Questions that can be used to reflect on the findings:
- What are these findings telling you about what is needed, and about what matters to different groups of respondents?
- Which findings confirm your assumptions?
- Which findings challenge your assumptions?
- What is new or surprising for you?
- Which new questions have surfaced for further inquiry?

Step 4. **Embrace change and take action**

To build a link between data reflecting the past and action in the future, focus on facilitating discussion asking, 'what can we do now?' The following questions can be used to reflect on the findings:

- Where in the visual pattern (on the triad or along the slider) would you like to see more responses in the future, and where less? Why?
- What do we need to do to move the responses toward this desired future or away from an undesired state?
- What do we need to do differently?

Logistics

Organizing collective interpretation events requires dedicating time to ensure that presentations, handouts, and materials are ready, that an appropriate venue is found, and that any services needed have been contracted. The ideal venue is spacious enough for collective and creative work, and to place flip charts for collective visualization group work. Participants should be invited well in advance and provided with any necessary information.

For the event content, ensure that there are printed copies, USB drives, or shared folders of the following:

- Detailed agenda for the event
- Signification framework used to collect the narratives and facilitate their self-signification
- Annotated presentations, flip charts, or posters with preliminary findings to be discussed
- Handouts with information that is considered important for collective interpretation, such as the SenseMaker purpose and learning questions, or the analytical framework, and the theory of change used as part of the design
- Selected story packs from respondent groups of interest
- If there is time and money, a brief overview and background of the SenseMaker process purpose, objectives, and key preliminary findings.

Documentation

What is specific to SenseMaker is documenting the sometimes quite unexpected analytical processes. Insights emerge, questions surface for possible further inquiry, and conclusions and decisions can suddenly be made. These need documentation to ensure the events are of optimal value. It is particularly important to keep track of where insights come from, as it is easy to forget the analytical logic or the combination of variables that led to a specific finding. Having a competent person responsible for documenting all group and plenary discussions is thus vital, as the interpretations and insights are the main value of the collective interpretation. Assigning people to be responsible for group documentation and one person as a coordinator to organize the material will help keep the sensemaking process on track.

Building Block 3: Comprehensive Analysis

Comprehensive analysis complements primary analysis and is an important building block of the Sensemaking phase. It can add significant value to the findings and insights, contributing to the process and enhancing actionable insights. Whether, how, and when comprehensive analysis is used all depend on the purpose of the SenseMaker process, the communication plan, and the expertise and resources available. If the core team decides that comprehensive analysis will be conducted, it will be important to plan for it during the Preparation phase and to include it in the plan for the Sensemaking phase.

This section describes ways to approach comprehensive analysis, focusing on the value that it can add and the different analysis pathways that it can take. It offers some practical examples but does not aim to be an exhaustive guide to data analysis. Comprehensive analysis requires the participation or support of people with skills in quantitative and qualitative analysis, and who also have practical knowledge and experience in the use of the non-SenseMaker analysis software summarized in Table 28.

While the boundaries between primary and comprehensive analysis are subjective and study-specific, a useful way to think about this difference is to look at the following dimensions of the sensemaking strategy discussed earlier:

- Analysis approach
- Type of data use
- Analysis techniques
- Combination of software used
- Degree and nature of stakeholder participation.

These are discussed in more detail in the following sections.

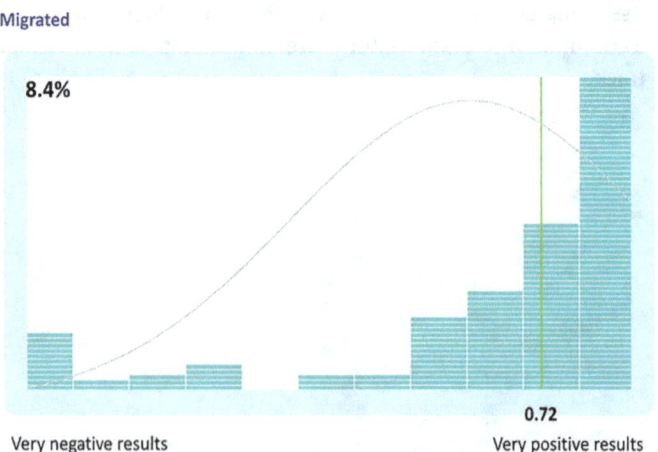

Figure 16.
Responses to migration as a coping mechanism when faced with a shock or stressor (Gottret 2017)

Taking a more structured approach to analysis

How exploratory or structured will the analysis be?

Purely exploratory — Purely structured

Comprehensive analysis can be used to further explore the data in response to a specific learning question or part of the analytical framework. It can also be used to respond to questions that emerge during primary analysis. Comprehensive analysis requires a more focused or guided approach than does primary analysis.

For example, observations that emerged from primary analysis of resilience study data showed that 8.4 percent of respondents migrated to cope with a shock or stressor that put their lives or livelihoods at risk, and that this coping action tended to yield positive results (Figure 16). In this example, comprehensive analysis focused on exploring this insight further, in order to understand why people reported that migration yielded positive results. The starting point for this was to map the analysis pathway, as shown in Figure 17.

Shifting the focus from pattern visualization to in-depth narrative analysis

How much focus will be placed on pattern detection or narrative analysis?

Only pattern detection — Only narrative analysis

Comprehensive analysis may involve shifting the focus of analysis from visual patterns and exploratory narrative analysis to an in-depth analysis of the narratives (see Box 12). This may require the use of different software packages. For example, NVivo and Atlas.ti have been used for qualitative text analysis (Table 28), and R for quantitative text analysis and visualization.

Figure 17. The analysis pathway: role of migration

1	2	3	4
Create a subgroup of respondents who have migrated to cope	Within this subgroup, create three categories for those respondents who had positive, neutral and negative results	Calculate the percentage of respondents in each group	Extract narratives for each group and conduct statistical text analysis of each story pack

Box 12.

Different ways of using narratives in comprehensive analysis

In the Guatemala example, an issue for further inquiry was flagged when staff participating in collective interpretation were surprised to see that—contrary to expectations—respondents reported having good outcomes from experiences that involved migration. A decision was made to examine texts in order to better understand why these respondents coped by migrating, and what happened in the experiences that yielded good results. To do this, story packs from respondents who had a positive migration experience as a coping mechanism (responses on the right-side of the pattern with a value of 0.72 or higher) were selected.

Looking at this narrative subset showed that migration was chosen as a last resort to avoid a loss of income or assets, mainly because of crop (maize and bean) failure due to drought, and the high incidence of leaf rust that decimated coffee plantations. Destinations varied; some were in the country where people could work as daily workers or rent land to plant, while others were in neighboring countries, such as Mexico or Costa Rica. A significant number cited the United States. Migration experiences were described as hard for both the person who left and for those who remained, and the most difficult experiences involves those who went to the United States. However, people self-signified these experiences as positive because the income they gained allowed them to cope with the loss and enabled them to provide for their families, despite the challenging situation. In many cases, they returned with money to invest in agriculture.

Another example is from the assessment of 17 years of agriculture and livelihood programming in Nicaragua. A slider was used as a proxy for the desirability of an experience. Respondents were asked if they felt their experience should be repeated or occur more often, or if they never wanted it to happen again. Pattern visualization and collective interpretation showed that there was a strong cluster of respondents who never wanted their experience to be repeated. The question was: Why?

Narratives from the respondents with answers in this cluster were extracted, imported into NVivo, and analyzed. A word tree (Figure 18) that uses a branching structure to show how selected words are connected to other words showed that these respondents had lost part or all of their harvest due to climate-related problems: drought, erratic rainfall, and rust disease triggered by a changing climate. As a result, these households had either no surplus to sell and could not repay their loans, ending up indebted, or they could not produce enough to eat and had to buy food to meet their needs. One major coping mechanism of these families was to sell their labor as farm workers or to migrate temporarily.

Switching focus to more comprehensive pattern visualization and statistical analysis

How qualitative or quantitative will the analysis be?

Pattern visualization and qualitative narrative analysis

Statistical data, pattern and narrative analysis

Comprehensive analysis may involve shifting the focus from visualization and basic exploratory data analysis to more comprehensive visualizations and statistical data, pattern, and narrative analysis.

This approach to comprehensive analysis may include:
- Collapsing data into new categories and creating new variables for additional exploratory analysis or statistical analysis.
- Understanding the relationships between elements across different signifier questions, in order to identify commonalities in how respondents tend to answer these questions.
- Evaluating whether the differences observed between subsets are statistically significant.

Figure 18. Qualitative analysis of narratives: word tree. CRS, Nicaragua

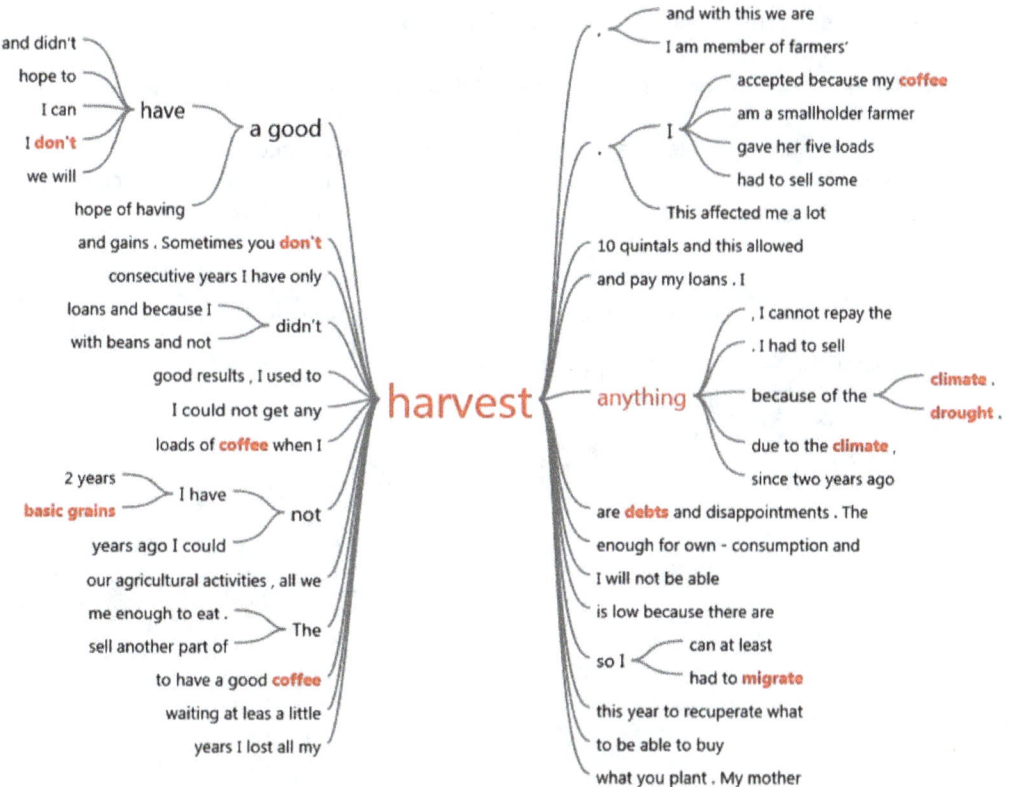

Collapsing data into new categories

Primary analysis and collective interpretation may prompt the need for further inquiry about subsets of respondents that were not considered during the Design phase. Due to this, MCQs that would help in comparing these subsets of respondents were not included in the design. To address this, a new categorical variable is created by collapsing data into new categories.

For example, in the resilience-focused CRS study in Nicaragua (see Box 12), a slider with stones was used to capture data about how respondents felt before and after the experience they shared in their narrative, and how they currently felt. The responses were placed on a line along a spectrum from 'very vulnerable' to 'very prosperous'. Initial results (Figure 19) showed there was progression from feeling more vulnerable before the change process to feeling more prosperous after it, and even more prosperous by the time the interviews were conducted (June–July 2015). Another question in this signification framework generated data that suggested that although, on average, farmers followed a prosperous pathway, there were those in the sample who did not.

Combining responses to these two questions during primary analysis allowed identification of six trajectories: (1) good and stable; (2) progressing; (3) resilient (rebounded or rebounded better); (4) vulnerable (rebounded worse); (5) regressing; or (6) stagnant. During the comprehensive analysis, this observation was reintroduced into a dataset as a new variable with six response categories representing each of these pathways (see Figure 20).

Understanding and visualizing the relationship between different concepts

Primary analysis and collective interpretation may point to a need to analyze relationships between different variables for the overall sample, or just for specific groups. This can be undertaken statistically (regression analysis) or through visualization.

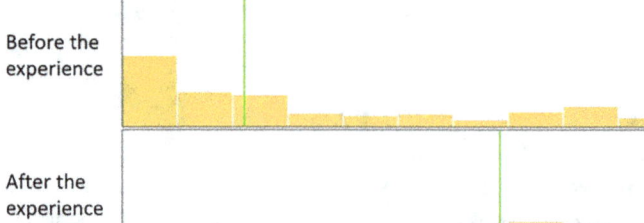

Figure 19. Respondents' progression along a 'pathway to prosperity'

For example, the CRS team in Nigeria explored the relationship between the effects of loans and savings and the levels of self-sufficiency. They looked at a subset of respondents who self-reported as members of a savings and internal lending community (SILC) group. The two concepts were present in two separate framework questions—a canvas-with-stones signifier question and a slider signifier question, with self-reporting membership of the SILC group captured by an MCQ (see Table 40).

To determine whether there was any observable difference between how SILC members responded, compared to SILC non-members, the team created two XY plots in Analyst (in what is now called Workbench)—one for SILC members and one for SILC non-members. These XY plots are scatter plots, where one dot represents one respondent's position along two variables. They show the association between the effects on loans and savings and the level of self sufficiency (see Figure 21).

Working with comprehensive visualization: density plots

Where there are many data points, scatter plots (like those in Figure 21 below) and ternary or triangular plots can become difficult to read. In this case, they can be converted into density plots, constructed by running a kernel density estimation (KDE). Some examples—contour map and heat map—are provided in Figure 22.

These plots help to demonstrate clusters and potential outliers, which is useful for comparing different populations. They enable a comparison of the likelihood of a specific combination of variables occurring together, relative to any other combination on the same plot (see Box 13). Density plots can be produced in R or in any other statistical software that supports visualization capabilities.

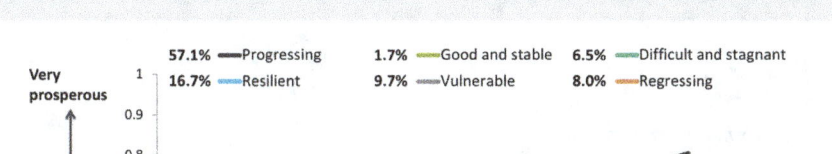

Figure 20. Post-categorization of trajectories along a 'pathway to prosperity' (CRS, Nicaragua)

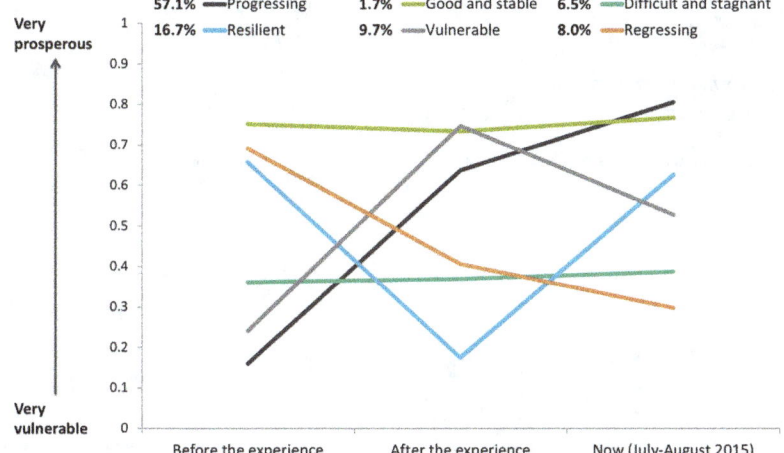

Table 40. Signification framework questions to explore link between effects of loans and savings and levels of self-sufficiency

Select no more than three resources that were most related to the experience you shared. Place each one in the space below to show if they had a positive or a negative effect on your ability to care for your children and to show how your access to each one changed over the last year.

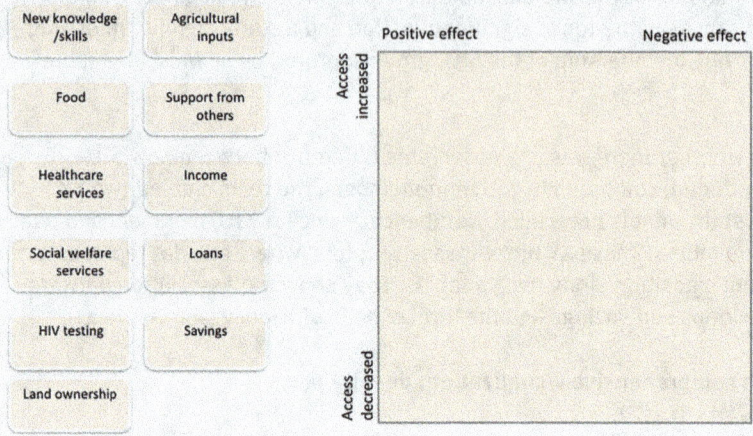

This experience made you feel...

Completely dependent on others — Completely self-sufficient

In the past year, what groups did you participate in? *(Select all that apply)*

- ❏ Religious group
- ❏ SILC group
- ❏ Other community savings group
- ❏ Infant and young child feeding group
- ❏ Caregiver forum
- ❏ HIV support group
- ❏ Men's or women's group
- ❏ Farming group
- ❏ Community improvement team
- ❏ No response

Figure 21. Exploring the relationship between two variables

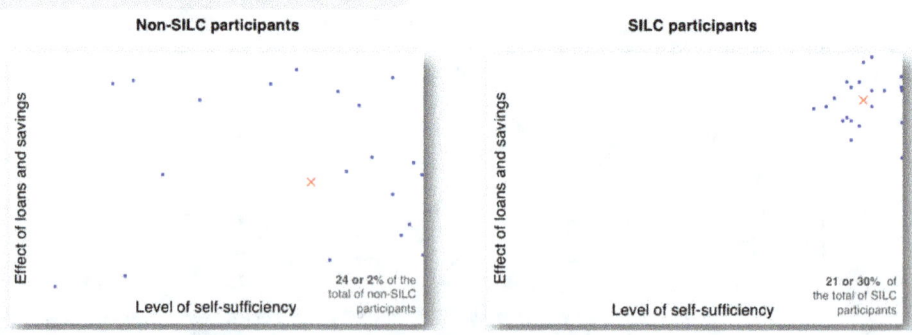

Figure 22. Examples of density plots: contour and heat maps

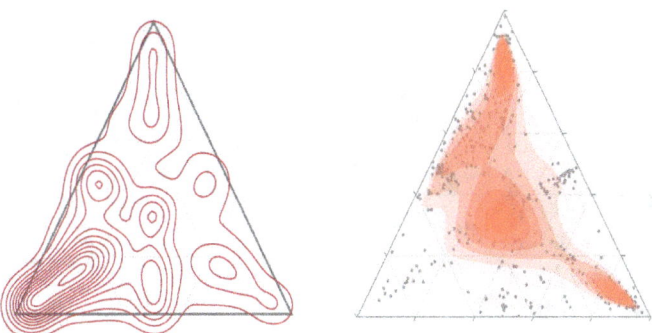

Box 13.

Using visualizations to explore relationships between two variables

Continuing with the example of migration as a coping strategy, the question was raised during collective interpretation of whether there was any association between the results of migration as a coping strategy and changes in income. To answer this question during comprehensive analysis, Analyst (in what is now called Workbench) was used to generate the XY plot in Figure 23. This shows that the respondents who had a positive experience of migration also had a positive change in income. In addition, Stata was used to estimate the Pearson correlation coefficient between these two variables, resulting in a positive correlation of 0.30.

A scatter and a contour plot were also produced in Analyst (in what is now called Workbench) (Figure 24). The contour plot showed two distinct clusters of respondents: those who experienced a positive result from migration and a positive change in income (upper-right corner) and those who experienced a negative result from migration and a negative change in income (lower-left corner). Narratives of the latter subset were read to better understand why these respondents had such negative experiences, and to explore what could be undertaken to support them.

Figure 23. Exploring the relationship between two variables: XY plot

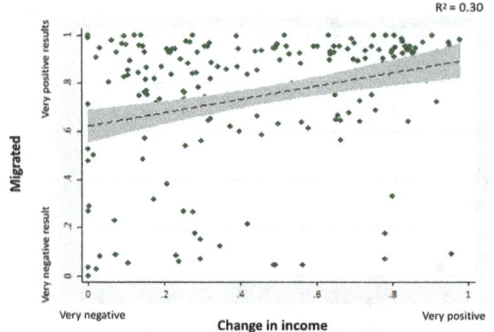

Figure 24. Exploring the relationship between two variables: contour plot

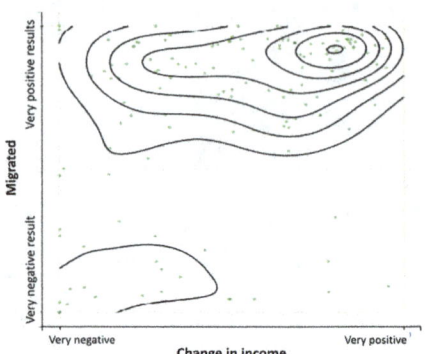

Figure 25. Filtering a slider question by the pathway followed

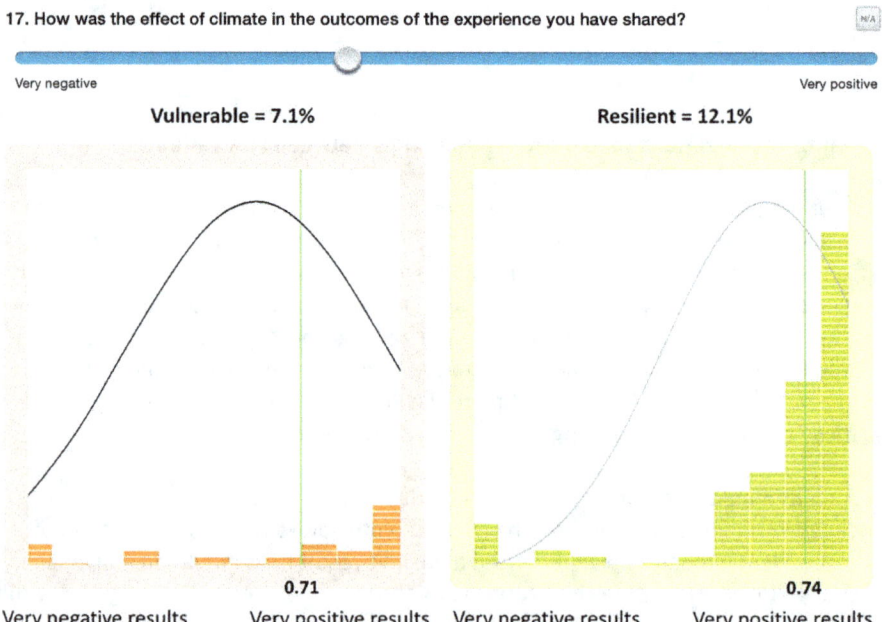

Determining whether the differences between two groups are statistically significant

Primary analysis and collective interpretation may lead to further inquiry of whether the differences between groups are statistically significant, providing more robust conclusions about differences in visualized patterns or percentages based on MCQ responses.

For example, in the CRS multi-country study on resilience, a question for further inquiry emerged during primary analysis and collective interpretation: Did respondents who had experienced a resilient pathway tend to have a more positive experience with migration than those who experienced a vulnerable pathway? To answer this question, a new categorical variable was generated, as explained in a previous section (collapsing data into new categories), and the slider question was filtered by the pathway followed (the new categorical variable). The resulting visualization (Figure 25) shows that respondents who followed a resilient pathway tended to experience a more positive result from migration as a coping mechanism than those who followed a vulnerable pathway.

However, visualizations cannot verify if such a visual difference is significant. If statistically sound sampling techniques have been used, it is possible to apply statistical analysis in the form of a t-test, as part of comprehensive analysis, to reach more robust conclusions. In this example, the t-test showed that the difference in the outcome of migration as a coping action between respondents who followed a resilient and a vulnerable pathway is statistically significant.

Moving from The Cynefin Company's proprietary software to third party software

Comprehensive analysis may require the use of software other than that used during primary analysis. For example, during primary analysis, the core team may visualize triad response patterns and compare these across regions using Dashboard, while during comprehensive analysis, R may be used to generate density plots, R or Workbench to explore the relationship between different concepts (XY plots), R to run text analysis, and Stata and SPSS to explore relationships between variables. In addition, comprehensive analysis may require documentation to proceed differently to that used during primary analysis.

What software will be used?

Only SenseMaker software — Mix of specialized reporting analysis and software

Scaling down to a smaller core team

Moving from primary analysis to collective interpretation often involves broadening participation to a larger number of diverse stakeholders. However, given the time and skills involved, these will then need to be scaled down to a smaller core team, or in some cases to a single individual, for comprehensive analysis. The core team may need additional analytical expertise not found in the core team, and only for a specific analytical task. For example, if during primary analysis the core team generated triad response patterns and compared these patterns across regions, comprehensive analysis may then involve an individual with statistical analysis or subject matter expertise probing further in order to establish more detailed or robust conclusions.

Building Block 4: Communication and Use

Progress updates and results that emerge during the SenseMaker process need to be communicated to different groups of stakeholders, if they are to be understood and have any impact. This includes updating the core team throughout the process, producing briefing notes and interim reports for stakeholders, and documenting and communicating the objectives and the process for a wider community.

This section focuses on how to communicate SenseMaker findings to audiences for whom this method is new, who may disagree with the findings or methodology, or may find it hard to take action based on the findings. Specific aspects of SenseMaker offer the potential for overcoming challenges but may also make communication and use more difficult. For example, SenseMaker is complex to explain methodologically, but its many visual aspects can greatly aid understanding of the findings. This short section will only focus on SenseMaker-specific aspects, not challenges common to other methods.

Good communication ensures that the results surfacing from the analysis and interpretation of SenseMaker data find their way to those responsible for acting on them. Ultimately, the purpose of all this sensemaking work is to make decisions about what to do (and not to do) next. If the evidence suggests that work is going well, are there activities that can expand the reach of these successes? On the other hand, if the work is not going as well, should some changes be made to the plans, strategies, or interventions?

Communicating negative findings

Reporting negative or sensitive findings is always a challenge. However, negative findings are opportunities for learning and improvement. The sensemaking process is focused on viewing all findings—surprises, in particular—as sought-after areas for exploration. Communicating frequently throughout the sensemaking process can help ease the acceptance of findings, whether critical or not. Try to share preliminary findings with stakeholders early to discuss the implications for action. Frequent communication reduces the element of surprise, should negative findings surface. Share all findings as opportunities to reflect and engage in dialogue. When negative findings are presented as an opportunity for learning, they can be seen as part of the process of identifying solutions to challenges, rather than as failings.
As SenseMaker is still relatively new and unfamiliar, people who do not like the findings may well find fault with the method. SenseMaker can challenge assumptions in sometimes very confronting ways. Do not be surprised if findings that challenge assumptions are met with skepticism and methodological critique.

Communicating weak signals

The visual power of SenseMaker lends itself to making weak signals visible. These can be important analytical aspects to communicate, helping to broaden people's minds away from only thinking of dominant patterns and averages. Significant weak signals can be illustrated with a visual of the question, to show where they are visually positioned in relation to other data points. They can be supported by additional data from stories linked to those data points.

Message development and prioritization

SenseMaker produces a great deal of interesting data, but charts and graphs alone do not help with learning or inform decisions. What are the emerging storylines and main messages? Revisit the communication strategy developed during the Preparation phase. Identify which key messages or findings should be shared with which audience. When developing key messages, use only the most relevant data: the ones needed to tell the story. Additional findings can be annexed, so that those who wish to pursue an issue further can find information there.

Supporting focused messages or storylines with relevant data does not contradict the open inquiry of the sensemaking process. Main messages or findings can clearly be supported by data, and still keep a conclusion open for exploration.

Not all findings in a sensemaking study carry the same weight. Some should have greater implications than others. But, just as too many data sets can become a useless recitation of information, so also can a cacophony of messages.

To help order key findings, address the weightiest and most significant first. Organize key messages according to their importance. Keep in mind that the significance of the findings may vary depending on which audience is being addressed. Good communication means taking the time to signify key findings.

A call to action

The insights revealed by the sensemaking process have the potential to greatly affect projects, programs, and more — but only if they are acted upon. Do not miss the opportunity to urge audiences to action, to take the next step, and to go even further. Ask 'so what does this mean for you?' and 'now what can best be done?' If action from the audience is needed, request it and ask for a time frame.

Understanding, ownership, and use are fostered by the active involvement of sensemaking stakeholders from beginning to end. It is both the process and the products of sensemaking that help ensure the call to action is answered.
It is a good idea during sensemaking events to work toward an action plan, aimed at responding to specific findings of the SenseMaker process. This emphasizes the actions that are of greatest priority based on the evidence.

Use narratives to tell the story

SenseMaker narratives can do more than simply serve as data points. Consider illustrating a key message or study finding with a representative narrative from one of the respondents. Stories may be memorable in ways that numbers are not. Never violate privacy, never use narratives for which respondents have not given consent to share, and never use information insensitively.

Communication channels

The sensemaking process should identify what, when, how, and to what extent findings should be shared. But it should also consider how information might be received and used. Today's swift flow of information makes clear, concise, and useful communications imperative. It also demands going outside the comforts of convention when reporting sensemaking findings.

Once content has sharpened into focus, consider the variety of vehicles that can or should deliver the information to the intended audiences. The most successful communication efforts use a variety of channels to get the messages across to the right audiences. Box 14 lists options to consider.

Visual communication

SenseMaker data and findings lend themselves to visual presentation and pattern visualization. Make the most of known good practice:

- Be selective. Beware of visual overload. It is easy to muddle the audience with graph after graph. Only share data that will be most relevant to the audience and communicates the main messages.
- Be aware of the audience's information needs. Select what to present through the lens of the audience's needs and interests. How will the audience use the information?
- Give answers, not just data. A visual image should provide an audience with streamlined information. It should stand alone and provide information that is easy to grasp.
- Minimize text. Too many words on a slide defeats the purpose of visualizing data.
- Consult chart guides to determine the chart type that is most helpful for the data to be displayed. One is available from Extreme Presentation (Chart Suggestions — a Thought-Starter).

Check for clarity

SenseMaker can easily be communicated with too much jargon, unnecessary complexity, and endless streams of data. Before finalizing any communication, whether for collective interpretation or as a final output, ask:

- Has the use of jargon been minimized or avoided?
- Is the language clear and simple?
- Have the writing and visuals been edited, and then edited some more?
- Is the material culturally sensitive to the audience?
- Are the messages, recommendations, and lessons clear, relevant, targeted, and actionable?
- Have quality photographs been included to add visual and emotional impact to the key messages and findings?
- Does the audience know how to get in touch through a range of channels, such as email, phone, website, and social media?

Box 14.

Channels to communicate SenseMaker findings

Traditional reports detail the full scale of the sensemaking study and often include an executive summary, explanation of methodology, findings, recommendations, and conclusions.

Face-to-face meetings offer unparalleled opportunities to share and discuss findings with key stakeholders. Seminars, conferences, workshops, and presentations for key audiences can effectively communicate sensemaking findings and create fertile ground for action.

Mini-reports or briefs summarize the key findings and can range in length from one to over four pages. They are often developed with the understanding that the intended audience lacks the time or patience to comb through a full-length report. The advantage is that they can be quickly and seamlessly adjusted to suit the information needs of different audiences. They highlight only the core findings and messages to the appropriate audience.

Journal articles share key findings of sensemaking studies with niche audiences, as well as influential ones.

Media outreach through press releases, press conferences and, increasingly, social media is appropriate when findings should reach a broader, public audience

Websites and web portals. Place studies and evaluations in an online clearing house that can be accessed internally for learning purposes. In addition to your own organization's website, consider posting findings on other collaboration and learning sites. An online audience generally wants information fast. Summaries that are simple and accessible are better suited to this medium but can provide links for deeper information. Make the most of the opportunity by introducing the work with a short synopsis that will catch the reader's attention.

Social media. An OECD survey in 2016 (Zimmermann and Gregoire-Zawilski 2016) found that development communicators chiefly used social media to communicate results of their agencies' work. The social media networks used were, beginning with the most popular, Facebook, Twitter, YouTube (also Daily Motion, or Vimeo), blogs, Flickr, and LinkedIn. Social media can communicate visualized findings to intended audiences in a powerful way. Consider what is most available and most accessible. Brevity is key.

Fast facts and postcards. Distil key results and messages into a series of one-page fast facts or postcards. Turn these into snappy displays for print or online. Use them on websites and blogs, and in tweets.

Epilogue: Why We Wrote This Guide

Steff Deprez

In 2008, I was working for Rikolto Indonesia in an Inclusive Business program for coffee, cacao and rice. As the Coordinator for Planning, Learning and Accountability (PLA), I was searching for methods to help us listen better to smallholder farmers. I came across SenseMaker and was immediately attracted by its different way of working with stories. I initially used SenseMaker as a workshop method with large groups of smallholder farmers and immediately felt its power: capturing real-life experiences, self-interpretation, quick pattern visualization showing the diversity in perspectives and triggering debate and insights for action. When I shifted to a global PLA role in Rikolto (2010), we invested in SenseMaker and developed the Inclusive Business Scan. At that time, SenseMaker was new in international development. We experimented our way forward with how to organize the different stages of a SenseMaker process and experienced the diversity of possible applications.

When I started working independently in 2013, I was fortunate to be involved with several SenseMaker projects that expanded the interest in international development, including Girl Effect (then Girl Hub), Care USA, CRS, IFAD, ESF and Via Don Bosco. At that time, I learned a lot about applying SenseMaker in MEAL processes. SenseMaker brings the day-to-day experiences of people to the forefront and the diversity of their perspectives and realities. The method allowed us to hear people's voices at scale with an open lens rather than being constrained by pre-defined indicators and targets. I saw how using SenseMaker touched practitioners at a level that changed their perspective on programming and their MEAL practice. I worked closely with CRS for some years as they built internal capacity, embedded SenseMaker in their M&E and research and started to document the process.

Intrigued by the philosophy and uses of SenseMaker and other narrative methods, I founded Voices That Count in 2017, a collaborative network of practitioners and consultants that use narrative decision-making and sensemaking approaches for social impact. Where we initially used SenseMaker for MEAL purposes in international programmes, we use it now in support of citizen participation, citizen science, participatory action research, context scans, strategic planning, adaptive programming and policy formulation. Writing this guide together was an enormous learning process in itself and has further shaped my thinking and practice. I hope it will support first-time and experienced users to enhance their practice and that it will inspire people to explore and innovate further with the method.

Maria Veronica Gottret

In my search to make relevant contributions to development practice, I expanded my career from a technical degree into economics and social sciences research. This was also a transition from mainly using quantitative research methods to using mixed method approaches to better understand social relations and norms, and especially human behavior. These aspects have a profound influence on our capacity to generate desired development outcomes and goals. Convinced of the need to place these issues at the center of development practice, I embraced this career path when I joined the International Institute of Social Studies (ISS) in The Netherlands to pursue my PhD in Development Studies. There the available suite of qualitative research methods inspired but also challenged me greatly. I used life histories to understand smallholder farmer innovation and see development interventions through their eyes, with semi-structured interviews to understand development interventions from different types and levels of development practitioners' perspectives. I was fascinated but also overwhelmed with documenting, analyzing and interpreting the very rich data collected.

Being an innovator by nature, I had the privilege to be part of a team at Catholic Relief Services (CRS) with exceptional leadership who were convinced that development practice deals every day with complexity. Six years ago, they gave the space and resources to learn and test the SenseMaker method. The first pilot was like love at first sight, though the journey had many hurdles and detours, as any organizational innovation. But being on the ground, listening to the narratives of the people we are aiming to serve has been the most enriching experience in my whole career. Reading hundreds and thousands of these narratives while analyzing patterns and quantitative data as well, generated as part of the self-signification process that the method facilitates, showed me its power to dig deeper into the root causes of the events or symptoms than other evaluation and research methods. Furthermore, engaging CRS and partner staff in collectively interpreting the findings for adaptive program implementation showed me the value of the findings and evidence it generates to take informed and effective action to improve the lives for those served by CRS. After this six-year journey of developing my expertise with SenseMaker, I look back to my years as a PhD student at the ISS and wished I would have had SenseMaker in my research methods suite.

Irene Guijt

In 2007, I was deeply frustrated by the limitations of the M&E toolbox that I had at my disposal. In my work, I had noticed how we were working like blinkered horses, only looking at what we knew we needed to know. What about all the unexpected insights that emerged in day-to-day chats? How could I break out of the prison of predetermined indicators that failed to accommodate the inevitable changes to success? How could I still hear, but at a scale that made it impossible to dismiss people's experiences as 'anecdotal' evidence? And how could this be undertaken with respect for people's own voice and choice?

Then in the last months of writing my PhD, I bumped into Kurtz and Snowden's article - I still remember the recognition and excitement. This led me to the early days of The Cynefin Company's work with SenseMaker in 2008. I felt like a child in a sweetshop! Finally, here was an option to 'listen to voices at scale' – the focus of the very first AEA presentation in 2010 on SenseMaker that I gave on my first attempt in a GlobalGiving pilot with John Hecklinger. And what a steep learning curve it was! There was no written guidance and no international development experience from which to learn. Since those early days, my experiences have been greatly transformed by advances in digital technology and hyperconnectivity. I moved from paper to tablets, from having people in Singapore develop the collection tool to designing the signification frameworks myself, from cursing over crashing software to being fully online, from fumbling in the dark about how to analyze these very different question types, to seeing the exciting innovations led by others.

When work started with CRS on SenseMaker in 2014, little did we know what a wealth of experiences would emerge, which greatly informed many aspects of this guide. Veronica has been at the forefront of all of this. To quench our collective thirst for clarity, coherence, and consistency, we started putting on paper the tacit knowledge that had largely been shared by word of mouth up to that point and my initial brief notes. It is deeply satisfying to see 'the art and science of SenseMaker' debated and now documented in such detail. It is my deep hope that it will inspire many others to innovate with ways to listen better to people who have so much to offer and so much to gain— and yet are often not heard.

Anna Hanchar

I am a social science researcher and I often use SenseMaker as an approach for investigating human behavior, social interaction and decision-making of real people in the real world – the complex world.

A graduate degree in economics and PhD in strategic management prepared me well to undertake methodologically robust research. More than a decade ago I moved to the private sector to deliver research projects aimed at bringing societal and business value. In this work, I developed an interesting but challenging agenda focusing on investigating dynamic, unpredictable and multi-dimensional problems that occur in complex systems. However, I soon realized that I was lacking the tools and approaches that would allow me to successfully tackle such problems.

I was intrigued when I first heard about SenseMaker as a 'complexity aware' approach and I embarked on a journey of learning about it. Now, years later, I am working in the field of social impact and sustainable development, and I often use SenseMaker approach to support projects in international development and social responsibility – locally and globally.

SenseMaker is a dynamic approach that continuously evolves and develops. When used correctly, and when it fits the purpose, I find it helps to deal with multifaceted phenomena and generates real value to stakeholders at multiple levels.

Rita Muckenhirn

After working for about thirty years in the development sector at the local and international levels, I was quite frustrated by all the attempts to capture evidence of very complex topics, such as social and behavior change, gender, participation, governance, peace and conflict.

When CRS asked me to join their SenseMaker pilot process, I was curious and simultaneously hopeful, though with some reservations. Once I started working with the approach, I not only became convinced of it, but now I would highly recommend using SenseMaker in any project to get deeper insights and to connect with people's voices. Listening to people's experiences and their way of reflecting on the meaning of their stories, being able to visualize patterns, to explore tendencies, strong and weak signals, to find surprises and interpret together with them the findings, and discussing how to use the results have become passions for me. The SenseMaker approach really makes sense to me, because it helps us to generate evidence and connect with people's lives at the same time.

My purpose in the future is to learn more about social and behavior change, as well as peace and conflict transformation, with this very unique and innovative SenseMaker approach.

References & Further Reading

Béné C, Frankenberger T and Nelson S. 2015. Design, Monitoring and Evaluation of Resilience Interventions: Conceptual and Empirical Considerations. *IDS Working Paper 459.* IDS: Brighton, UK. p. 26.

Boulton JG, Allen PM and Bowman C. 2015. *Embracing Complexity: Strategic Perspectives for an Age of Turbulence.* Oxford University Press: Oxford, UK.

Broniecki P and Hanchar A. 2017. Data Innovation for International Development: An Overview of Natural Language Processing for Qualitative Data Analysis. IEEE Proceedings of the 2017 International Conference on the Frontiers and Advances in Data Science (FADS): Xi'an, China.

Brooks N, Aure E and Whiteside M. 2014. Final Report: Assessing the Impact of ICF Programmes on Household and Community Resilience to Climate Variability and Climate Change. p. 96.

Casella D, Magara P, Kumasi TC, Guijt I and Van Soest A. 2014. The Triple-S Project SenseMaker Experience: A Method Tested and Rejected. Triple-S Working Paper 9. IRC: The Hague, The Netherlands.

CGAP. Insights into Action.

The Cynefin Company. SenseMaker.

Cognitive Edge. 2014. Using SenseMaker to Understand Girls' Lives: Lessons Learnt from Girl Hub. Girl Hub.

CRS. 2016. *Introducing SenseMaker: Giving Voice to Those We Assist.* Methodology Brief. CRS: Baltimore, US. October 2016.

CRS. 2018. *Capacity Strengthening SCAN (csSCAN): Instruction Manual.* CRS: Baltimore, US. September 2018.

CRS. 2018. Tangible Benefits to Child Wellbeing Seen Among Households Participating in Savings and Internal Lending Communities (SILC). CRS: Baltimore, US.

Deprez S. 2015. *Voices that Count. Using Micro-Narratives to Organise Systematic and Real-Time Feedback on the Inclusion of Smallholders in Modern Markets.* VECO: Leuven, Belgium.

Deprez S and Guijt I. 2021. *Can Voices at Scale Really Be Heard? Reflections from Ten Years of Innovation with SenseMaker.*
In: Burns, D, Howard, J and Ospina, SM. (eds) (2021) The SAGE Handbook of Participatory Research and Enquiry. London: SAGE Publications Ltd.

Deprez S, Huyghe C and Van Gool Maldonado C. 2012. Using SenseMaker to Measure, Learn and Communicate about Smallholder Farmer Inclusion. Vredeseilanden/VECO: Leuven, Belgium. July 2012.

Deprez S and Van den Steen T. 2016. Voices that Count: The Inclusive Business Scan (Powered by SenseMaker). VECO: Leuven, Belgium.

Frankenberger T, Landworthy M, Spangler T and Nelson S. 2012. Enhancing Resilience to Food Security Shocks. White Paper. Tango International: Washington DC, US. p. 57.

Frankenberger T, Mueller M, Spangler T and Alexander S. 2013. Community Resilience: Conceptual Framework and Measurement Feed the Future Learning Agenda. Westat: Rockville, MD, US. p. 49.

Gottret MV. 2007. *Rural Innovation and Smallholders' Livelihoods: Modes of Intervention in Hillside Communities of Latin America.* Shaker Publishing: The Hague, The Netherlands. p. 331.

Gottret MV. 2017. *Understanding and Assessing Resilience.* Methodology Brief. CRS: Baltimore, US. September 2017.

Gottret MV, Guijt I and Muckenhirn R. 2017. *Was Agricultural Livelihoods Programming a Pathway to Prosperity in Nicaragua? Lessons Learned Using the SenseMaker Methodology.* CRS Study Report. CRS: Baltimore, US. January 2017.

Gottret MV and Kast N. 2018. *Making Sense of Refugee Support: Using Narratives to Evaluate a Program to Protect and Integrate Refugees in Ecuador.* CRS Study Summary. CRS: Baltimore, US. March 2018.

Gottret MV, Muckenhirn R and Nyemba J. *Resilience Assessment Report: Budikadidi Project, Democratic Republic of Congo.* USAID and CRS: Baltimore, US, January 2019.

Gottret MV, Mureithi P and Mbokothe G. 2017. *CRS Farmer to Farmer Program: Building Resilience.* CRS Study Brief. CRS: Baltimore, US. September 2017.

Guijt I. 2015. *Guidance Notes for Story Collection (Interview/Paper-Based).* Notes provided during SenseMaker workshop. CRS: Baltimore, US. February 2015.

Guijt I. 2016. Innovation in Evaluation: Using SenseMaker to Assess the Inclusion of Smallholder Farmers in Modern Markets. In: S Bell and P Aggleton. *Evaluation in Health and Social Development: Interpretive and Ethnographic Perspectives.* Routledge: UK.

Guijt I and Hecklinger J. 2010. *Making Sense of SenseMaker: Evaluating Development Initiatives through Narrative Capture and Self-Tagging in Kenya.* AEA Conference, November 2010.

Jenal M and Hanchar A. 2016. *A New Framework for Assessing Systemic Change in Katalyst: The Pilot Study in Local Agri-Business Network.* [Shortened version available here]

Johnson A, Gottret MV and Muckenhirn R. 2020. *Making Sense of Gender Norms and Behaviors and their Implications for Food Security and Livelihoods: Girma Project Gender Analysis Report, Niger.* USAID and CRS: Baltimore, US. April 2020.

Kurtz CF and Snowden, DJ. 2003. The New Dynamics of Strategy: Sense-making in a Complex and Complicated World. *IBM Systems Journal*, 42(3): 462–483.

Kushal N and Sharrock G. 2015. Presentation: *Story Collection Training for SenseMaker Pilot.* CRS: India. April 2015.

Kushal N, Sharrock G and Andretta A. 2014. *Responding Effectively and Sustainably in Meeting the Needs of Communities. SenseMaker Pilot Survey: Story Collection Training and Field Testing.* CRS: India. April 13–17, 2014.

Kushal N, Sharrock G and Andretta A. 2015. *Responding Effectively and Sustainably in Meeting the Needs of Communities. SenseMaker Survey of Experiences in India.* Guidance on Data Collection. CRS: Baltimore, US. May 2015.

Lundy M, Amrein A, Hurtado JJ, Becx G, Zamierowski N, Rodríguez F and Mosquera EE. 2014. *LINK Methodology: A Participatory Guide to Business Models that Link Smallholders to Markets.* Centro Internacional de Agricultura Tropical (CIAT).

Guijt, I and Mager, FR. 2017. *Agile research in the risky realities of the Central African Republic.* Oxfam Real Geek Blog.

Mager FR, Smith R and Guijt I. 2018. *How Decent is Decent Work? Using SenseMaker to Understand Workers' Experiences.* Oxfam Research Report. May 2018.

Mager, FR and Galandini S. 2020. *Research Ethics: A Practical Guide.* Oxfam Research Guidelines. Oxfam Research Network.

Merchan R, Gottret MV and McQuillan D. 2018. *Nutrition-Sensitive Agriculture in Guatemala's Western Highlands: Understanding People Perspectives using the SenseMaker Methodology.* Cracking the Nut Meeting, Antigua Guatemala, Guatemala. June 12–13, 2018.

Muckenhirn R. 2015. SenseMaker: *This Really Makes Sense. The Process, Step By Step. Methodology Guide for Pilot Project Impact Assessment in Nicaragua.* CRS: Nicaragua. July 2015.

Smith B, Boyce M and Mohammed Z. 2018. I am Determined to Realize my Dream: *Understanding Decision-Making During Displacement and Return In Iraq.* Oxfam Research Report.

Snowden D. 2010. Naturalizing Sensemaking, in Mosier KL and Fischer UM (eds). *Informed by Knowledge: Expert Performance in Complex Situations.* New York: Psychology Press. pp 223–234.

Snowden DJ and Boone ME. 2007. *A Leader's Framework for Decision Making. Harvard Business Review,* 85(11): 68–76.

Thagard P and Cameron S. 1997. *Abductive Reasoning: Logic, Visual Thinking, and Coherence.* Philosophy Department, University of Waterloo: Waterloo, Ontario, Canada.

Walker D, Samuels F, Gathani S, Stoelinga D and Deprez S. 2014. *4,000 Voices: Stories of Rwandan Girls' Adolescence. A Nationally Representative Survey.* ODI: London, UK.

Williams B. 2015. Prosaic or profound? *The Adoption of Systems Ideas by Impact Evaluation. IDS Bulletin.* 46(1), January 2015.

Zimmermann F and Gregoire-Zawilski M. 2016. *We Asked 13 DevCom Members about Social Media. Their Answers will Blow your Mind*! Presentation at DevCom Workshop, Paris. OECD. May, 2016.

www.ingramcontent.com/pod-product-compliance
Lightning Source LLC
Chambersburg PA
CBHW050413120526
44590CB00015B/1947